How to Be Happy

David Burton is an award-winning playwright and theatre director from Brisbane. He is best known for his plays *April's Fool*, *Orbit* and *The Landmine Is Me* (co-written with Claire Christian). *How to Be Happy* is his first book.

daveburton.com.au

HOW TO BE HAPPY

A memoir of love, sex and teenage confusion

DAVID BURTON

TEXT PUBLISHING MELBOURNE AUSTRALIA

textpublishing.com.au

The Text Publishing Company
Swann House
22 William Street
Melbourne Victoria 3000
Australia

First published in Australia by The Text Publishing Company, 2015

Cover and page design by Imogen Stubbs
Cover illustration by Louise Lockhart / Offset
Typeset by J&M Typesetters

Printed and bound in the US by Lightning Source.

National Library of Australia Cataloguing-in-Publication:
Creator: Burton, David J., author.
Title: How to be happy : a memoir of love, sex and teenage confusion
            / by David Burton.
ISBN: 9781925240344 (paperback)
ISBN: 9781922253156 (ebook)
Target Audience: For young adults.
Subjects: Burton, David J.
            Men—Australia—Biography.
            Depression in adolescence.
            Adolescence.
            Happiness.
Dewey Number: 920.71

All the events in this book are true. Only the names of the people have been changed.

I've Lied to You Already

I don't know how to be happy.

Yeah, sorry. Awkward.

Okay, let me rephrase. I don't know how to make *you* happy. But I have a pretty good idea what would help. Trouble is, my tips sound fairly lame. It's like when you ask someone about the secret to losing weight and they answer 'eat well and exercise'.

True, but profoundly unhelpful.

Also, I'm not a doctor, nor do I have any qualifications in psychology. I have qualifications in the arts, which means I can tell you how to critique a post-feminist interpretation of Shakespeare and how to fill in a Centrelink form.

Given all of this, if you're still feeling like you'll read this book, you're an incredibly trusting person. I like that about you. Seriously. You're friggin' lovely.

I'm writing about happiness because I'm obsessed with it. There are whole swathes of my life that have been completely absent of joy. I've been diagnosed with clinical depression on and off since I was a small child. As I grew into adulthood, I started to acknowledge that I had a pretty serious problem, and I sought ways to make myself happier. I guess you could argue that most of us are doing this all the time anyway—looking for happiness in all sorts of places: good marks, new friendships, booze...

But of course, as most of us know, true happiness and unlimited contentment are always available. You see, young padawan, true happiness is only ever found within yourself.

Yuck.

Lame. But true.

Here are some other big, broad things that research tends to point towards helping with happiness:

Sunlight. Go outdoors. Sunlight raises serotonin in the brain, which makes you happier. It's a natural antidepressant.

Exercise. Now look, I'm with you on this one. I've

got plenty of anecdotal evidence to suggest that exercise makes you quite *un*happy. It makes me grumpy and constipated. But once you get over that stage, you do feel unmistakably brighter. I'm reluctant to admit it, but exercise does make you happier.

A healthy social life. This one's always been tricky for me. I'm a fairly introverted guy at heart. But having a close network of friends and good relationships means you have a community to support you in times of need. I didn't have that, outside my family, for ages. Then I found it. More on this soon.

Eat well. Healthy in body means healthy in mind. Again, I can argue with this one. McDonald's three times a week makes me *very* happy. In the short term. But not in the long. Most of the time, a balanced diet helps a balanced brain. Bummer.

Okay, those are out of the way. You knew them anyway, right? They're common sense. I think we all *know* how to make ourselves happier, it's getting there that's the trouble. It's always been the trouble for me.

The only completely true, solid, non-lame advice I can offer is my experience. There have been times when I've been happy, and times where I've been dangerously unhappy. How can our stories ever be split into those two categories? Happy. Sad. My life, so far, has had an abundance of both, but never in a clean-cut fashion. I can't begin to separate the two out and try and tell you how to be happy just from my happy moments, or how to avoid sadness just from my sad moments. I have to tell you the whole darn thing.

Angel Faces

Meet Cameron. He has his hands around my neck, holding me splayed across a table in visual arts. The class is full of noisy kids who aren't really fazed by the fact that I'm about to die. It's only a couple of weeks into high school, but they're used to Cameron's antics.

The bohemian art teacher has only worked at the school for six months. In fact, she's only worked in teaching for six months. At the end of the year she'll throw in the towel on a career that was obviously never her idea in the first place. But right now she's standing on the opposite side of the classroom, uncertain what to do, as Cameron's hands grind tighter and tighter around my neck.

I provoked this attack when I said that Cameron was an idiot. In my defence, he was. Or, at least, he was acting like one.

I had muttered it in a cowardly manner, jeering back at him when he called me a faggot. In his defence, I was. Or, at least, I was acting like one.

Unlike Cameron, I couldn't catch a ball and I wasn't interested in the quantity of froth that could be produced from shaking a coke can for five minutes. I had proven adept at understanding some things that Cameron couldn't, however. Like basic maths and English. And so I was a faggot.

'I could snap you like a twig,' he slurred into my face.

I was used to bullying, and Cameron was the typical bully in every way. He was tall, had spiky hair, and he had received an extra kick of testosterone before a lot of the other thirteen year olds around us had. He even had a sidekick: Trent. Trent was the weakest kid in the whole of our year level. He was round, he feigned stupidity and he hero-worshipped Cameron. Unlike me, he had made a wise choice, early on, to make himself Cameron's best friend to prevent the inevitable arse-kicking that he would receive if he didn't.

Who had I made *my* best friend in the high-school game of thrones?

Dearest, darling Ray.

On the very first day of high school, I was standing outside a classroom, waiting for class to start or for someone to give me orders.

'Do you like cheese?' said a deep voice from behind me.

I turned around and met Ray. We proceeded to have a ten-minute conversation about cheese. We resumed it over lunch. And then we picked it up again the next day.

I would come to both despise and love Ray. He was my instant ticket to the bottom rung of the social ladder, but he didn't judge me. As long as we were talking about cheese or *Pokémon*, I was an amazing friend.

It took Ray slightly longer than most people to get his sentences out. He had long, greasy hair, which he tied in a messy ponytail. His skin was shiny and unwashed, and his clothes sat on him like they'd been thrown on from a distance. There were no lockers at our school, which meant that we carried the day's textbooks around with us. So the new students were weighed down by a bag almost as heavy as themselves. But Ray seemed more weighed down than everyone else.

Ray had Aspergers. I diagnosed him within seconds and immediately felt comfortable. I knew Asperger's Syndrome intimately through my younger twin brothers.

I suppose I should try to explain Aspergers. It's not easy.

Have you ever been a sober person at a really messy party? Around you are loads of people having fun, singing and making out, occasionally stumbling over to you and slurring nonsense in your ear. There are moments of lucidity, maybe even enjoyment, when their drunkenness doesn't matter and you're able to feel part of the fun. There are other times where you feel completely alienated from the madness around you. You might even feel that you're in significant danger, and you're being driven towards an anxiety that no one else can understand, as they're too busy riding high on something that you're not a part of.

That's kind of what being Aspergers is like. It's not a brilliant explanation, but it's a start. There are countless others.

My favourite is an unconfirmed story I heard long ago that originates in the nineteenth century somewhere. It's said that people with Asperger's Syndrome tend to have innocent features, with gentle contours and unblemished skin, sometimes described 'otherworldly'. (It helps to think of the elves from *The Lord of the Rings* here.) This, combined with their general demeanour, led them to be called 'Angel Faces'. This title is still around today. Search 'Aspergers' and 'angels' and you'll get a myriad of sites that claim theological proof that people with Aspergers are reincarnated angels.

I like this bizarre deduction, not for its validity (although whatever floats your boat is fine by me), but for the idea that there is nothing inherently *wrong* with Aspergers kids. It's not them who need to learn from everyone else; it's *everyone else* who should learn from *them*.

But I fear I'm not getting any closer to an explanation.

Asperger's Syndrome is, fundamentally, a social and communicative disorder. Asperger's Syndrome kids have a great deal of trouble connecting with the world. They find it extremely difficult to read emotional or social cues. The subtle signals that we use everyday to demonstrate how we're feeling can be completely lost on them. To survive, many learn to mimic emotional states.

Aspergers folks have a low threshold for stress and anxiety. So things need to stay in a strict, predictable routine. If that routine is broken even slightly it can lead to an unforgettable trauma.

My brothers were born two years after me, and diagnosed with Asperger's Syndrome some time before they were five years old. The doctors originally thought they would never speak. This turned out to not be the case, and the twins have grown up to be, in most ways, functioning members of society. But it is unlikely that they'll ever have jobs, and they stay at home, full-time, with my parents.

What makes my brothers effortlessly charming is their coping mechanism. They can, at will, recite any of the following television programs in their entirety: *Family Guy*, most of *The Simpsons*, *Thomas the Tank Engine*, *Friends* and *The Adventures of Lano & Woodley*. In addition, their video-game library spans an entire wall. Ask them to recite any scene from these and you'll be met with an incredibly enthusiastic monologue.

For a long time when they were growing up, ninety-nine per cent of what the boys said came directly from a film or television show. Their dictionary was pop culture.

Feeling angry? Their voices would flatten, deepen and take on the exact intonation of Homer going off at Bart. Disappointed in somebody's naughty behaviour? The Fat Controller would suddenly possess them, and they'd give a lecture to a 'very naughty engine'.

Over time, they've found their own voices. These days they can articulate their inner-emotional states without resorting to television shows. It's the result of a lifetime of hard work.

So I grew up with Frank Woodley, Colin Lane, Peter and Stewie Griffin, Chandler Bing, and the Fat

Controller. Somewhere in there are Andy and Chrissy, my brothers.

Cue sentimental indie acoustic guitar, and enjoy the following montage of my life, growing up.

Chrissy is six when he collapses in the backyard. He is breathing and his eyes are open, but he's completely unresponsive. Desperately worried about some kind of brain failure, Mum throws him in the car and we rush to hospital.

Upon arrival, Chrissy wakes up from his catatonic state and immediately goes back to playing. Mum nervously interrogates him, and Chrissy mildly replies, 'I was Superman, affected by Kryptonite.' His commitment to the role was stunning.

Mum plans an innocent surprise for Dad. A professional photograph of his wife and three children for his desk. It's a nice thought: Andy, Chrissy, Mum and me all beaming at him. But the teenage photographer lacks the social skills to deal with the twins, who are not up for being told where to sit and how to smile or being ordered to keep still. They're only six or seven. The result of half an hour of failed photos is a tantrum from both of them. It's exceedingly public. Mum eventually gets them into the car. Just before she drives off, someone knocks on her window.

A woman smiles condescendingly as Mum rolls the window down. 'Hi,' she says to Mum, 'I couldn't help but notice you were having some trouble. I wanted to let you know that Jesus may be able to provide answers for you.'

The boys chastised Mum for swearing so much at the young woman.

At a primary school concert, Andy and Chrissy become the stars of the show. Their flawless rendition of a *Lano & Woodley* skit is met with wild applause. When they sit down to watch the others perform, however, they turn into harsh critics. They can't understand why everyone else isn't capable of perfection. A pre-teen amateur girl band squeaking out the *Pokémon* theme song is met with a particularly disgusted sneer from Andy.

When the girls bound up to him to ask him what he thought, he doesn't pause before responding: 'You sounded like crap.'

We have a conversation about manners on the way home.

'But they sounded like crap!' Andy argues, his skin becoming red and itchy in frustration.

In his defence, they really did.

We're very young when we're playing in the backyard of a friend's place. Desperate to be liked, I'm doing my best to join in. One of the older boys suggests that we grab some tomato sauce and trick the twins into thinking we're bleeding. The plan goes like this: we'll run into them, fall over, and then blame them when blood starts going everywhere. The plan goes off without a hitch. The twins are confused and distraught. The older boy thinks I'm a hero. I hate myself.

Woolworths. The deli counter. In an effort to encourage life skills, Mum asks Chrissy to order some meat.

'Hi,' Chrissy says confidently to the girl behind the counter, 'Can I have a dozen chicken vaginas?'

It's a line from *Family Guy*.

The girl quietly calls her manager.

We're at a party shop buying balloons in bulk. Chrissy grabs a fake rubber bum and proceeds to the counter.

'Hi,' Chrissy says with a smirk to the young girl behind the counter, 'Can I have a new butt? This old one's got a crack in it.'

It's a line from *Family Guy*.

I grab Chrissy before the girl can call her manager.

The weird thing is, this is my normal.

Reactions vary when I tell people about the boys, but a common feature is pity.

'Oh,' they say, 'that must have been so hard for your parents.'

Yep, it was damn hard. They had to make some tough decisions, and I think they raised two remarkable young men.

It took me a long time to realise my brothers were different. As a young child, I thought we were normal. Three kids, two parents, a cat and a dog. The picket-fence family.

Then something mysterious happened when I was twelve or thirteen. I got a lot of hair very quickly, my voice started cracking, and I became ultra-aware of the world around me. I had always wanted to be liked, and I'd always cared what people thought of me, but now my world expanded, and I suddenly realised just how different the twins were. We couldn't take a family photo. We couldn't go on adventurous holidays. We couldn't try out a new restaurant or new food. Routine was a religion in our family. Spontaneity was blasphemous and would almost certainly lead to tears.

Imagine building this world while also raising *another* neurotic young man. My parents did an amazing job under tough circumstances. They did their absolute best for me. I was never denied an opportunity. But there was a lot that was inevitably impossible for my family. And when I became a teenager, I began to resent all the ways we were different.

As it turns out, this feeling of resentment is a fairly normal part of being a teenager, Aspergers in the family or not. Everyone thinks their family is about as cool as wearing socks with thongs. Everyone feels their family is probably the daggiest bunch of dags ever to have bred.

But just as strong as the resentment is the fierce and loyal protection that only brotherhood can summon. I felt this for Ray too. Bullies picking on me was one thing, but making fun of the truly defenceless was abhorrent.

Not that Ray would need that much protection. Ray knew every single line from *Austin Powers* off by heart. By the end of year eight, he would be celebrated for his talents. His sense of humour would even disarm Cameron.

∧∧∧

We should get back to Cameron.

'I could snap you like a twig,' he slurred into my face.

'Yes, you probably could,' I replied through his tight grip.

Cameron, intellectual that he was, was baffled by my response. It wasn't what I was supposed to say. I was supposed to put up a fight which would egg him on further. I was supposed to retaliate physically and provide him with the opportunity to display his manliness by bashing me into a fine paste. Sadly for him, he wasn't prepared for the idea that I was a coward. Perplexed, and wearing an expression not unlike a bewildered animal, he let me go.

It was the first week of high school, and it was not going well.

I had somehow stumbled out of a primary school, a world I understood and knew, into a place rich with stereotypes. It was like I was in a cartoon. There was the Aspergers kid with the cheese. The bully with the spiky hair and chubby sidekick. The handsome boy from South Africa who everyone had a crush on. The girls who practised dance routines at lunch and made mean comments to each other. The boys who kept their shirts untucked and refused to wear the school hat because they were just that *cool*. The first-year teachers who were overwhelmed and tried not to cry in the face of harsh adolescent rudeness. The experienced teachers who smoked between lessons and hated every one of us.

In this mess, who the hell was I?

I was too scared to have my shirt untucked. Too terrified to join in on girly dance routines. Too Australian to be a handsome South African.

I hated it. But I really didn't want to hate it. I wanted to be calm, cool and confident. It would do no one any good for me to whinge and whine. This was high school. It was part of growing up. And I needed to get on with it. This was my opportunity to be a man and show my family that I was ready to be an independent young adult.

So when Mum picked me up every afternoon and asked me about my day, I would say 'fine'. Reassured by this, Mum would then tell me about her day. I didn't want to tell her the truth about Cameron or my feeling of intense isolation, because Mum had a lot on her plate.

Our family was changing. At that time, we lived fifteen minutes outside town, across the road from the tiny country primary school that I had attended. Andy and Chrissy still went there, and Dad taught there too. My high school attendance meant Mum and I would drive into town everyday, with Mum frequently staying there for work. (I did try the bus at one stage, but the smoke-filled, noisy, forty-five minute trip home added an extra two hours to the day and added opportunities for Cameron to point out that I was a fag. I begged Mum to drive me back and forth.) The splintering of the family—Mum and me in town, Dad and the boys back home—was creating some pressure.

Importantly, the time for the boys to move into high school was just two years away. How would they handle adolescence? Where could they go? The tiny primary school had been perfect for them, but there were no high schools nearby. It meant a change was coming, and change is the enemy to the Aspergers mind. Would they be able to survive the confusing mess of classrooms, teachers and bullies?

Some minor cracks were appearing in my parents' marriage, and Mum would share her worries with me. Dad felt alienated from Mum, and Mum felt under-appreciated. I tried to give advice, but I was incapable of understanding the true depth of their adult problems. Both Mum and Dad were dealing with their own life-long battles with depression. Mum would often cry in those days. I recognised in Mum a vulnerability that was also in me: a desperate, heart-wrenching loneliness. With few friends to turn to and a lack of family beyond her children and husband, Mum found solace in her eldest son. I tried to be the best support I could.

On the evening of Cameron's attack, I went to bed shaken. The thought of returning to school the next day made me want to vomit. I had avoided a beating, but I was certain I wouldn't be so lucky next time. At lunchtime I would hide in the library, but there was no way I could avoid Cameron in class.

As I lay there, something else that had been bothering kept coming to my mind.

At high school, who was I?

In primary school, I'd been a friendly kid with a small bunch of reliable friends.

In high school, I was the loner who spent the day in desperate fear.

Quiet tears soon became loud sobs. The noise was enough to notify my parents.

'What's wrong, buddy?' Dad asked.

I quickly tried to think of a lie. Um...Rachel and Ross just can't get it together on *Friends*?

But I had never cried over television.

Ummm...

Palestine?

But I had no actual knowledge of Palestine.

I had nothing. I could only tell the truth.

'I hate high school,' I sobbed.

Mum and Dad held me.

'Buddy,' Dad said, 'you've been saying it's fine.'

'You should tell us these things,' Mum added.

I felt awful. I was worrying my parents unnecessarily. Why couldn't I just toughen up?

The next day, Mum apologised for sharing her marital problems with me. I promised her it was fine, genuinely wanting to at least *know* the path to my parent's divorce (that's how it looked in my mind). So Mum continued to talk to me about all sorts of things that I didn't understand.

It was clear to me then, and even clearer to me

now, that Mum was determined that I wouldn't feel unloved or uncared for in comparison with my brothers. The private school, the new uniforms, the car drives in—the whole thing was about me being given every opportunity that I could be afforded. Mum and Dad were making sure that I never missed out on anything because of the twins.

On top of all this, Mum committed a crime that is universally feared by all teenagers: she interfered in the intricate social balance of school. To my teachers, I had been the fairly quiet nerdy kid who hung out with Ray. But a hastily made phone call the day after my weeping soon turned me into the unhappy quiet nerdy kid who needed urgent help because he was a big wimp.

I knew nothing about Mum contacting the school until a morning assembly, when my English teacher (who I'd only had one lesson with) approached me.

'You're in the debating team,' she said, as though it had been settled years ago. 'Come to the meeting at lunchtime.'

I was scared out of my mind. But I went. A teacher had given me an order.

This teacher was Mrs Coates. She would change my life forever.

2

Smeghead

Mrs Coates was awesome and super-hot in an I'm-a-thirteen-year-old-and-you're-a-young-pretty-teacher kind of way. She was an English and drama teacher, and a very decent costume designer. She came to school in colourful and daring fashions that soon got her into trouble with the rest of the staff. Tops with bare shoulders, shirts with rock music logos, and impressive boots with big heels. For her subtle subversion of the rules, she got immediate respect from us all.

As instructed, I met Mrs Coates in her classroom at lunchtime. She smiled warmly as I came in. Her red lipstick was especially shiny that day.

'David,' she said. 'Welcome. Have you met Simon?'

She gestured to another boy on the other side of the room. Simon looked too sporty to be in debating. He was solidly built and had short, shaved blond hair.

'Hi,' he said confidently.

'Hey,' I replied.

'So,' Mrs Coates began, 'we need a debating team. We meet once a week, write our speeches together, and then we have a debate about once a month. I've got you both in different English classes and I think you'd be great.'

Oh, God. I wanted to stand out *less* at high school, not do anything that would make me stand out more. I especially didn't want to try to work with a sporty kid like Simon. He didn't look like he'd be into debating at all.

'Good evening ladies and gentlemen,' I imagined him saying in front of our entire year level. 'Today, we're debating the question: Is David Burton gay, or just a woman? As first speaker, I will be making the point that he's quite possibly both, and should be exiled from society as soon as possible.'

I blinked back to reality.

'We can't really proceed just at the moment,' Mrs Coates was saying. 'We need at least three. So consider your first week of homework to go out and find a third speaker. I'm sure you'll track down someone.'

I thought about Ray trying to be a debating speaker. I couldn't imagine him being interested in much else aside from *Pokémon* and cheese. But I didn't know anyone else to ask. This was going to be a disaster.

'Is that all right?' Mrs Coates asked Simon.

I looked to him. For the first time I noticed that he was holding a gridded notebook and an expensive graphics calculator. We weren't supposed to buy those things for another couple of years. Maybe I'd read him wrong. Maybe he was nerdier than I thought.

'Yeah,' he said.

Mrs Coates moved her beautiful blue eyes to me.

'You're fine with that, aren't you David?'

I swallowed. I smiled. I couldn't disappoint her.

'Yes,' I said. 'Absolutely fine.'

∿∿∿

High school subjects were weird. None more baffling to me than manual arts. A room full of sharpened blades and automatic power weapons was apparently the perfect place to put a mob of restless teenagers.

Cameron was unusually good at manual arts. He burnt a perfect penis into the side of his ash tray. My ash tray failed to meet the sole criteria of an ash tray: holding ash. In fact, it couldn't hold anything. It looked like a slightly bent scrap of metal.

Our next assignment was a doorstop. The final test was a disaster. I watched as the classroom door easily moved my miserably chiselled stick of wood, slamming shut on it and snapping it in two. My poor doorstop never stood a chance. Cameron saw the whole thing, of course, and applauded. In my imagination Cameron was the door. I was the malformed and useless doorstop, snapping pathetically under his force.

It was in woodwork that the blood came. I was chiselling far too enthusiastically at my block of wood when I was given reason to pause. Heavy drops of dark red were pooling on top of the timber.

I raised my hands. My right hand was covered in blood.

'Did you cut yourself?'

This question came from the girl across the table. Mary.

Mary was known throughout the school for her muteness. She was a round-faced, sad-looking girl, who tucked her shirt into her skirt and pulled it up, higher than her waist, to cover her slightly overweight midsection. Her short brown hair covered her freckled face, and her eyes, if you could manage to see them, were remarkably large and wide, open with quiet terror. I had been watching her from afar ever since the school's open day last year, when she stood at the back of the classroom and cried as the principal welcomed us all warmly. We were all uncorrupted and shivering twelve year olds then, without uniforms, and without a pecking order. Mary stood at the back, head up, looking forward, not moving, with tears slowly rolling down her face.

In the months since then, her tears had stopped, but she remained mute and afraid. We had been thrown into each other's orbit by social order alone, drawn to the same wood-shop table in silence.

This was the first time I had heard her speak. Her voice was soft, delicate and full of concern. I looked at her in surprise.

'Did you cut yourself?' she asked again.

'Um, no. I don't think so. I don't know.'

Then Mary pointed to my chest, right at my heart. She smiled. I had never seen Mary smile. In surreal wonder I looked down at my shirt. A pool of red ink was spreading across my pocket. The realisation came to me instantly. The red pen in my pocket was leaking. Cameron had given it to me outside, insisting that I carry it or he'd punch me in the dick. Without thinking, I had put it in my pocket.

Mary and I laughed.

I'd found my best friend.

∧∧∧

Mary joined the debating team. Simon hadn't found anyone. Mrs Coates was very pleased to welcome Mary on board.

Basking in Mrs Coates' tuition and her gentle warmth and positivity, Mary's confidence blossomed. And mine did too. I found the one lunch hour a week I had with Mrs Coates a wonderful respite from the classrooms and the terror of lunchtime.

Plus, I enjoyed debating: articulating well-defined points, making an audience laugh to bring them round to your side. All of it clicked with me. It was the best part of high school.

My first impression of Simon had been all wrong. Sporty wasn't quite the right word. Simon was tough and determined. He looked at home in his perfectly ironed uniform, and his hair never seemed to grow past the clean tidiness of his buzz cut. Simon treated high school like it was the military. He wanted to succeed.

Simon was smart. Super smart. Smart in a way that I wasn't. Our maths classes came together later that year. I was completely lost in maths, but Simon was at home. He was more than willing to help me; he talked me through my mistakes. The situation was reversed in English. I found a similar pleasure in pointing out nouns and verbs and subtext to him.

Simon was confident but a loner. We were

diametrically different men. He was the science guy, and I was the artist. In life outside school, we would never be companions, but our desperation drove us together. We were mates. Along with Mary, we were a regular Three Amigos.

As our friendship grew, school slowly became easier. It also helped that towards the end of the year, Cameron was expelled when he gave someone a blood nose and a teacher found pot in his backpack. I never saw him again.

After twelve months, it seemed I had finally been able to answer the question that had so perplexed me since I arrived: who the hell was I? I was the debating guy, with the two friends. We were 'that' group. We went to the library most lunchtimes. Simon and I swapped computing magazines. Mary and I memorised and acted out British sketch comedy. To put it bluntly, we were big nerds. But we didn't really care. Nerds are the best people.

My new community had come at a cost. Ray faded into the background. I remained kind to him, and he would occasionally sit with us at lunch, but he was difficult to talk to and sometimes unintentionally rude.

'What's that?' he would say with disgust, looking down at a humble ham sandwich Mum had packed for my lunch.

I shrugged. 'Just ham,' I said.

'No cheese?'

Cheese was Ray's favourite thing in the world. It was cheese, *Pokémon* and *Austin Powers* with Ray. That was his entire world.

I shook my head. 'No. No cheese.'

'You're an idiot.'

This was a clear and serious accusation from him. It wasn't a joke. I really was an idiot. He even seemed personally insulted that Mum hadn't put cheese on my sandwich.

Simon slapped Ray sharply on the back of the head. 'Who asked you?'

'Hey!' Ray yelled, as Simon laughed at him.

Even though I could see the slap had hurt, I laughed too.

'Stupid dickhead,' Simon said. 'What are you, a freak? Not everyone has to like cheese.'

Ray was silent. I could see he was hurt. If Ray and I had been on our own, I would've tried to explain to him that calling people idiots is probably not a great idea. But it had felt so good to have a friend stand up for me.

'Yeah, freak,' I said.

I selfishly believed I had filled my Aspergers quota. Our lunches often became about Simon calling Ray names and telling him to shut up.

I never stood up for Ray. He stopped hanging out

with us at some point. We didn't go looking for him.

With Simon and Mary, life became brighter. Mum and Dad's apparently inevitable divorce never came. The tensions seemed to dissolve as the year settled down. Mum and Dad still battled with depression regularly, but I was concentrating on other things.

Mary and I discovered Harry Potter together, which, in terms of major life events, is almost as important as YOUR ACTUAL BIRTH. Lunchtimes regularly involved rushing to the library to pore over the latest instalment in Harry's adventures and attempting to make predictions about upcoming books. We would also discuss *Star Wars*, *Hitchhiker's Guide to the Galaxy*, *Discworld* and *Doctor Who* at length. We were nerd soulmates.

There are few reasons I would ever wish to be a teenager again, but I could be persuaded if it meant rediscovering all of these stories again for the first time and finding my unabashed passion for them. I didn't realise it at the time, but I was joining a fraternity of teenagers that had existed since the 70s. The socially awkward, tragically unathletic, deeply intelligent teens. Lean, gawky and uncertain, we were destined to cling to the sparkling wonders of fictitious worlds as if they were lifelines. They *are* lifelines. They offer an escape from a world that has declared war on the introvert. Schools relentlessly celebrate outgoing students, catapulting the contemplative introvert into group work, team-building and utter hell. While our genetically gifted extroverted counterparts found their freedom on the sports field, Mary and I found it inside our own heads, in rich worlds that were infinitely witty, imaginative and heartbreakingly not real, in spite of our ardent longings to the contrary. How we wished we could escape to a faraway planet. This collective imagining was the greatest feat of romance I could imagine.

Simon, meanwhile, taught me chess, but only in a way that meant that he would always win. A lot of our conversation was based on competing with each other. We became fierce rivals in politics. Simon's family was staunchly conservative; they eyed my family's liberal-ism with suspicion. Mary would watch on as Simon and I did battle over Australia's immigration policy.

'They're coming in to destroy our country!' Simon would yell at me.

'They're coming in because they're running *away* from their *own* destroyed countries!' I'd yell back, outraged that he could be so callous.

'You'd believe anyone's sob story.'

'You've got no heart.'

It would have been so much easier if we were less interested in the world and could've solved our constant competition for the alpha-male position by bashing each other behind the bike sheds.

I often found myself wondering how or why we were friends. It was a bizarre relationship.

Friendship with Simon and Mary made high school tolerable, but I yearned for greater acceptance from my peers, especially a few of the prettier girls. They never seemed to notice me, ever. To be fair, it's hard to notice someone who hides in the library playing the *Harry Potter* trading-card game while loudly exclaiming that Alexander Downer is a terrorist.

But I swooned whenever a girl dared to give me a smile. I was a sucker for the girls whose names sounded like they had come from a fairytale film.

There was Christine Pennyworth, whose endlessly cheery demeanour and kind words made my heart sing an opera and my mouth make socially inappropriate squeaking noises. And Danielle Rosen, whose hair matched her name. Danielle kept all the footy boys in line, and made them all show off for her, and she giggled all the while.

I needed something to get their attention, or any attention. I needed to show that I could be funny, and smart. I didn't want to go through high school as the quiet nerdy kid no one noticed.

I needed drama.

∿∿∿

Drama wasn't offered in the first year of high school, but I leapt at the chance in the second year. Mrs Coates was head of the drama department. She wrapped up our final first-year English class by asking me to stay back.

'You'll be joining me in drama next year, won't you?' she asked.

'Of course!' I replied. I was ecstatic. The more time with Mrs Coates the better.

I was not the only one who thought so. Mrs Coates was new to the school, but under her leadership the student numbers in drama absolutely exploded.

First class. First day. Theatre sports. You run into the space and make up a scene off the top of your head. You get embarrassed quickly, but if you get over yourself and just play in the scene, it's actually quite easy to be entertaining.

I was embarrassed every day. I was shoved into walls, called a faggot, and the target of countless spit balls—what did one more piece of humiliation matter?

With that uplifting thought, I stood on the side as two of my classmates began a scene. They were giggling, embarrassed as the entire class looked at them, waiting for them to be entertaining.

'Hi, um...Phil,' said one of the girls, before collapsing into a fit of laughter.

'Phil' could only laugh in response.

For some reason Phil was the funniest name anyone had ever heard.

'Focus!' yelled Mrs Coates from the back of the room. 'Find a way to introduce something new into the scene.'

'Phil' managed to restrain his giggles for a second to mutter: '...have you seen the cat?'

Well.

That was my cue.

I got down on my hands and knees and sauntered into the scene. The class broke out into a sudden explosion of laughter. I sat, licked my hand and groomed myself.

For the first time since I'd arrived at high school, my peers looked at me with respect. With my lips pursed and my bum in the air, I felt my heart swell. And from that day on, I was viewed very differently. I was given a sudden promotion up the social ladder.

I was as surprised as you are.

Every scene in drama became about how big or outrageous I could become. I was funny and unpredictable. I had dared to do what so many others had found too terrifying: to just *try*. I was no longer Faggy Nerdy Dave. I was Crazy Drama Dave. It was a role I wore easily and welcomed. And it wasn't long before it went beyond the drama class and into every part of my social life.

Everything became a performance. On a sports field I had been absolutely lost and would usually sit on the side trying not to get noticed. Now sport gave me regular opportunities to show off.

Forced to play soccer? I would run around the field commentating the action in an inappropriate and racist faux-Mexican accent.

Called a faggot? I'd put on a lisp and a limp wrist and flirt with the idiot that dared to mess with me.

Internally, I was a different person. I suddenly had the strength to get through the day. I was convinced I had learned a valuable lesson, and it was one I wanted to share.

Mary, still the social outcast, was experiencing great anxiety one afternoon after a bunch of girls had been mean to her about her weight.

'It's easy,' I said, freshly arrogant from my new survival strategy. 'Just don't be yourself. Be someone else. You've got to put on a show for people. That's the only way to survive.'

Mary nodded in mute acceptance.

Worst. Advice. Ever.

The Swimming Carnival

For New Year's Eve, in typical nerd fashion, Simon, Mary and I decided to stay up and watch a *Red Dwarf* (dorky sci-fi sitcom) marathon. Although exhausting, it was delightful, and one of the rare times I can actually remember behaving like a normal teenager at my house.

Partly because of the twins, and also because of my own shyness, visitors to our family home were extremely limited. Having my friends over was a rare occurrence in the high-school days. I felt comfortable with Mary, who understood family weirdness instantly and didn't begrudge the twins' eccentricities or worry about the sometimes chaotic kitchen, or the piles of dog poo out the front, or the smelly bit of carpet in the hallway where the dog frequently pissed, or the sewing room that was almost impossible to enter because of the stacks of hoarded fabric.

Mary's house had similar signs of oddness which made me feel right at home. Her stepfather had painted a mural of a misshapen horse on one of her bedroom walls and there were stacks of magazines and boxes in various corners.

When Mary was giving me the first tour of her house, she wouldn't look me in the eye.

I tried to reassure her. 'This is great!' I said.

She shrugged. 'It's all right, I guess.'

I sat down on her bed and looked at the horse on the wall. 'I can't believe your step-dad painted that whole thing.'

'Yeah,' she smiled.

'Do you get on with him?'

'Yeah, he's a good guy.'

I suddenly realised that I knew very little about Mary's family.

'When did he and your Mum get together?' I asked.

'About five years ago,' she said. Her eyes moved downwards again. She was picking at her fingernails. They'd been covered in glue from a boring Religion lesson in last period. She did it all the time. I could tell she was thinking, and I wasn't sure if I'd hit on a sensitive spot.

Then she looked up. 'They met at the Walsh Home.'

I was surprised. 'Really?' I said. 'The mental home?'

She nodded. 'Yeah. He was a patient there. She was a nurse. She ended up pressing for his early release. She said she'd look after him. They fell in love really quickly. It was all a big scandal.'

'That's amazing!'

Mary smiled. My head filled with questions. Before I could ask, we heard the front door open.

'Mary?' came a voice from the lounge room.

Mary's mum was home. In an instant, I saw Mary's body change. She looked down again, sighed, and took to her nails with a fresh fervour.

When I went home to my own mum later that day, I told the story of Mary's mother's mental marriage with excitement.

'Isn't it amazing?' I gasped.

Mum was immediately doubtful. 'Are you sure?' she asked.

'It's what Mary said.'

Mum's eyes narrowed suspiciously.

Mum has always acted quickly. It was only a matter of days later that she hung up the phone with an air of triumph. I muted *Doctor Who* on the television to find out what she was so pleased about.

'That was Mary's mother,' she said. 'It's a lie. They never met at a mental hospital. They met through work.'

Oh, God.

'You *asked* her about it?!'

Mum nodded, happy with herself.

'But Mum, don't you think she'd be embarrassed and not tell you? Isn't it the kind of thing that would be a family secret?'

'If it's such a family secret, then why is Mary telling her friends? Sounds more like Mary's making up stories to impress people.'

I didn't let Mum see that I thought she might be right. I was too embarrassed by her snooping. Now the whole thing seemed ridiculous.

But why would Mary lie?

The next day at school, while Simon and I ate lunch and Mary read a book, I asked her. I tried to do it sensitively.

'So, you won't believe what Mum did last night,' I began. 'She rang your mum and asked about the whole story of how they met.'

Mary's face instantly turned pink. Her eyes grew wide with fright.

I continued. 'And your mum said it was made up.'

There was a tiny pause before Mary laughed. Great, big, raucous laughter. 'Of *course* it's made up,' she said. 'I was just being silly.'

I laughed too, but I was confused. Had it all been some kind of weird joke? I started to ask more questions, but Mary just laughed in response. After that, whenever I offered to go round to her house, she made excuses about her parents wanting her to study. I didn't visit again.

Simon's house, which I visited often, was a tightly controlled domestic unit. Every space was tidy and wiped clean. Bedtime was strict. Evening prayer was essential. Simon's father was a looming and intimidating presence who banned Simon from watching 'inappropriate' television shows like *Queer Eye for the Straight Guy* and other programs that were 'obscene'.

Queer Eye for the Straight Guy was a reality show where a bunch of gay guys did a makeover on a messy straight guy. My parents and I thought the show was hilarious.

'It's disgusting,' Simon said when I tried to recommend it to him. I was pretty sure he'd never seen it.

I had little awareness about the differences between our families until Simon pointed them out, starting with the messiness of my home.

'Do you ever, like, *clean* the kitchen?' he asked.

'Yeah, of course.'

'It just doesn't look like you do.'

I looked around. I saw the kitchen through Simon's eyes. There was stuff *everywhere*. An industrial-sized tub of peanut butter on the bench. A large pile of bills and paperwork. Pet-food cans. A bowl of apples, bananas and pears, all at different stages of life.

'Yeah,' I muttered. 'Yeah, you're right. Sorry.'

My house was too messy. I added the complaint to my growing list of teenage resentments about my family.

~~~

The Three Amigos were not destined to have romantic couplings. Crazy Drama Dave was funny—cute, but not hot. Not having a girlfriend or boyfriend didn't seem to bother Simon and Mary a lot, but I was vocal about my desire for a girlfriend. I felt like I had spent most of my life longing for an intimate partner. It was a grand and impressive vision in my head. A romantic soulmate. Someone to share my deepest thoughts with. Someone who would convince me that I didn't need to perform or compete with them. Someone I could be at ease with. I imagined finding a person who could share the burden of my secrets: all my worst fears about no one at school liking me, or that my family was unusual and that I might be unusual too. Someone who could hear all of that and still love me.

It was now almost two years since that first drama class. It was exhausting being Crazy Drama Dave all the time. If I could just find this one brilliant person, my life would be better in every regard.

Plus, you know, I was horny. But more on that later.

So I went hunting for this mysterious wonderful soulmate who was waiting for me, somewhere.

Christine Pennyworth could have been that person. Always smiling, always smart, kind-hearted and funny.

Yes. I should ask Christine Pennyworth out.

I spent many lunch hours with Mary and Simon, making plans, trying to summon up the courage.

'Okay. All right,' I would begin. 'I'll just go over and ask her out. Now. Right now.'

Simon shrugged, sipping from his coke can. 'Yeah, okay.'

'Do you think?'

Mary looked up at me with those big eyes. She didn't eat or drink much at school. She just sat with a book in her lap. 'Sure, if that's what you want.'

'Or I could ask her out through a note. I've got English with her this afternoon, I could just pass...'

Why wasn't this easier? I had convinced myself by this stage that Christine was my one and only. We were perfect for each other. I'd imagined the wedding, the kids, a broad and bright future together. Her holding me at night and whispering, 'It'll be okay.'

Now that I look back on it, it's odd that I didn't imagine anything more explicit beyond cuddling. I don't know if it was because I hadn't seen enough porn then, or that I didn't have enough sexual understanding to grasp the idea that we might do *other* things to each other. I knew I was horny, but that was about as far as my imagination shook. I wanted to be comforted and held.

After weeks of dreaming and planning, I finally found the words to ask Christine Pennyworth at the swimming carnival. Why then? I couldn't tell you.

You see, the swimming carnival wasn't a great time. I'd never been super comfortable with swimming, but it had really all fallen apart in primary school. I had done my pathetic little twenty-five-metre race, coming in last with everybody patiently waiting for me to get to the end. In the change room afterwards, as I was getting dressed, my fellow male classmates took my clothes away from me and whipped my naked body with towels.

High school brought up the memories afresh. I couldn't think of anything worse than getting down to boxers, showing off my pale, skinny frame, diving into icy cold water and floundering around for fifty metres in front of the entire school. I imagined lovely Christine watching on and laughing at me flailing around in the water like a drunk ostrich.

In the weeks leading up to the carnival, I grew more and more anxious. The head of physical education was a woman called Mrs Darling. She was short, tanned and terrifying. Every week she would get up at assembly and demand FULL PARTICIPATION. Non-compliance meant detention. Supervised by Mrs Darling. The thought of being left in Mrs Darling's dungeon was enough for me to stop breathing.

So we all had to participate. At least one event each. Fifty metres freestyle was to be my event.

'It'll be fun,' said Simon.

Fun?! Mrs Darling certainly didn't seem to think so. God forbid we should actually enjoy ourselves at the carnival. There were so many rules. Get on the right bus. Wear sunscreen. Wear the right kind of hat. Support your house. Cheer. You must cheer. You must participate. Get undressed. Dive into the water. Try not to die.

My anxiety was great enough for me to complain to my parents. I was so wound up about the entire thing. I couldn't swim. I'd grown up in inland Australia. I'd splashed around in the surf on the Sunshine Coast, but I'd never shown an aptitude or much of an interest in actually learning to swim. My freestyle was all free and no style. I thrashed about like I was drowning. I quite possibly was, depending on the depth of the water.

'I just don't understand,' I said to my parents, 'why you would take hundreds of young people who feel awkward in their bodies, make them get down to their underwear and then swim in front of each other. If someone asked you to do that now, as an adult, would you?'

The next day I was in drama, pretending to be a jive-talking tree, when the call came over the loud-speaker.

It was Mrs Darling.

'David Burton to room 206, please.'

I'd never been called over the loudspeaker before. The whole class turned as one to look at me.

I tried not to look afraid. I tried to be casual. Mary gripped my arm, terrified that I was about to disappear into Mrs Darling's dungeon. I considered briefly yelling my ardent love for Christine right there. I didn't know if I'd ever see her again. I closed my eyes and took a breath. I tried to convince myself it would all be fine.

The walk from the drama classroom to room 206 was long. For a moment I considered running out of the schoolyard, but I knew the consequences would only be worse. I thought of Mrs Darling picking up a ruler and hitting me repeatedly. I would take the blows calmly, I decided, then run back to Mrs Coates and show her the bruises. Then Mrs Darling would be fired. And Christine would think I was super brave. And we would live happily ever after.

I knocked on the classroom door. Mrs Darling was

teaching a class of sporty year-twelve boys about anatomy. A bunch of them were giggling up the back.

'TIMOTHY STILES!' Mrs Darling's voice bounced off the classroom walls. 'Would you *please* stop playing silly buggers and get back to labelling your uterus properly?'

'Sorry, Mrs Darling,' came a shy mutter from Timothy, and they all went back to work.

The short Mrs Darling had just whipped a group of hulky seventeen year olds into silence. Her eyes flicked to me.

'You're David?' she asked.

I nodded.

'Come here.'

I'd never seen her up close. She had her sunglasses off. I had only ever seen her up the front of assembly, shouting commands.

She raised her voice to the class again. 'No talking while I chat with David, please,' she said. Some of the senior students looked at me. I could've died. What was this all about?

Mrs Darling lowered her voice again and looked at me.

'Your mother called me,' she said.

Oh, God. Oh God, oh God, oh God. Mum, why?!

'She mentioned you were worried about the carnival.'

I couldn't summon words. My face was turning a bright red from shame.

Then something remarkable happened.

Mrs Darling smiled.

'Listen, I make a lot of noise up there at assembly, because I'm trying to get the slackers involved, and I know you're not a slacker. So don't worry, okay? Just swim your race on the day and you'll be fine. If you're worried I can give you some lessons, there's a bus that goes out after school every Tuesday.'

She's suggesting I spend *more* time on this? No way.

She wasn't nearly as scary as she once was. But the message was clear. There was no way I was getting out of swimming at the carnival.

'Thanks,' I managed to squeak. And I walked back to class.

I didn't have an option. Now Mrs Darling *knew* me. Before I was just an anonymous scared kid. Now I was the boy who got his mum to ring up the teacher. Mrs Darling would be looking for me on the day. I would have to swim the race.

∿∿∿

The carnival day came. I felt like throwing up.

One of the first faces I saw at the pool was Christine's. She was in the house next to mine, and we sat across the aisle from each other and talked. She was friendly and bright, and she cheered loudly. Her hair caught the rays of the sun and made my heart jump. Talking to her made me forget the upcoming race for a little while. Mary and Simon were in houses that had to sit at the other end of the stands. I wouldn't get to speak to them for most of the day. That was fine by me. So far, the swimming carnival was way better than expected. I would be sitting next to Christine all day.

Simon stepped on the starting block with ease, and I let out a little cheer. He dived perfectly and glided through the water as if humans were born to do it. He swam to the finish. He wasn't first. He wasn't last. He was in the middle of the pack. Not notable in any way.

I was so envious I could've puked.

Seriously, I could've puked. Because my race was next.

Christine smiled. 'Good luck,' she said.

'Thanks,' I replied. I prayed that she would be too distracted to watch my inevitable death.

I stood on the starting block. I tried desperately to remember how to dive. My goal was only to finish *not last*. I didn't want people to wait for me, to have the whole school watch my pathetic effort. If I could do that, swim a perfectly average race and not be noticed, this would all soon be behind me.

The gun went off.

I hit the water like a dinner plate hitting concrete.

The sharp sting across my stomach was numbed by the shiver of cold that ran through me. My brain was working faster than my body. I tried to recover and began to plough through the water. My arms moved as if they were shovelling dirt. My legs kicked as if they were motorised. I tried to remember to breathe. I was getting mouthfuls of water as my limbs created chaotic splashes all around me.

It wasn't long before an ache filled my arms and legs. Surely I was close to the end. The next breath I tried to look around me. I was barely halfway. I could see the others steaming ahead of me.

Oh, God. This was it.

I went further, moving past halfway. My arms felt dead. Stars began to blink in front of my eyes.

I would have to stop. I wouldn't be able to make it. Mrs Darling would have to dive in and get me out. Everyone would see. Including Christine.

My head became light. Every breath seemed to come with too much water. I stopped dead, standing up in the pool. I was a dozen or so metres from the end. The last few swimmers were finishing up.

I heard Mrs Darling's voice shout out with a laugh, 'Come on mate, you're nearly done!'

The stars were becoming sharper. I'd already stopped for too long. People were starting to notice. I plunged back into the water and moved with the grace of a slug. I touched the wall.

I'd finished.

It was done.

But I felt like I was about to pass out. Mrs Darling was shouting at me to get out of the pool. The next race was already starting.

I lifted myself out, but then I couldn't move. I felt weird.

'I think…' I began, but no one was listening. I tried to walk back to my seat.

I passed Mrs Coates.

'Are you okay?'

'I think I…I'm seeing stars.'

She sighed. Shook her head. 'You did a good job, Dave. Don't worry about it,' she said.

I knew she wasn't disappointed in me. She was disappointed in something else.

'Sit down here. Have some water. I'll check back in on you in ten minutes. If you're still seeing stars, let me know.'

I nodded and sat down. My towel felt like a blanket, covering my hairy, skinny chest. I was suddenly overcome with hunger. I hadn't eaten for twenty-four hours because I'd been so anxious.

There was a muesli bar in my bag. I ate it slowly, and my body started to return to normal.

Mrs Coates checked back with me. 'You okay?'

'I hadn't eaten,' I said, smiling.

Mrs Coates smiled. 'Take it easy, yeah?'

I nodded. The races continued.

I was done. I was alive. And nobody seemed to care about the fact that I'd taken so long. I went back to my seat. Christine was just returning from the food stall.

'How'd you go?' she asked.

Oh, thank God. She hadn't seen.

'Fine,' I said, shrugging.

The gun went off again. Christine and I stood up and cheered together. It was the most genuine cheer I'd done all day.

Everything was okay. It was all over.

I don't know what explains my state of mind as the day drew to a close. Maybe it was the simple elation of relief, or the fact that Christine and I had talked for most of the day. It felt like we had survived something important.

I asked.

I dropped the question in casually, as we were packing up. Like it was nothing.

'Did you maybe wanna go out with me?'

She was startled, and she turned to see if I was serious. I shrugged, and smiled. I would've said something if I'd had the words, but all of my clever little stupid jokes that had managed to make her laugh all day had flown elsewhere.

'I'll think about it.'

I nodded, and my voice came out a high, ball-busting shriek as I said, 'Sure, yeah, you know, whatever.'

She turned me down very gently the next day, with a maturity and a kindness that was beyond her years and possibly a script written by her parents.

'I'm very flattered,' she said, 'but I think we should just be friends.'

I laughed jovially, as if the whole thing was hilarious.

'That's okay,' I said. 'I was joking anyway.'

Crazy Drama Dave didn't do heartbroken.

4

Self-sabotage

Christine was a no-go. I'd blown it.

I'd never kissed anyone, and with each passing birthday I began to wonder if I'd ever get the chance. I was fifteen. FIFTEEN. And no kiss. I may as well have been a monk.

But my attention was soon to be taken elsewhere. I can't remember when I first noticed that Mary had changed. I don't think there was any great revelatory moment, but rather a slow and gradual knowing.

Mary had marks on her wrists. Thin, red, angry scratches, ruled with mathematical precision.

'What's that?' I asked.

She pushed her sleeves down to cover the marks. 'Oh, I was cut by a rose bush.'

But the marks were still there a few weeks later. In fact, they looked fresh. When I asked her again, her face turned pink and she turned away. She was lying. I'd seen her lie before. I realised that I was beginning to pick at a darkness that I had known was there but was unable to comprehend.

Mary's moods became black and indecipherable. Mum tried to explain incomprehensible concepts like cramping and PMS, but it was all lost on me. I just knew that my friend was changing in unpredictable ways.

When I finally came to understand what the scratches were, I dared not tell anyone.

Mary was doing it to herself.

I was confused, and scared.

Mary promised that if I told her mother, my mother, a teacher, or even Simon, that she would finish herself off. She would kill herself.

This wasn't me thinking I would die from embarrassment at the swimming carnival. This was *real*. I took Mary seriously.

I was the only person who knew. I set about trying to stop her from her slow mission to self-destruct.

The wrong word at the wrong time would send her hurrying to the girls' toilets with a blade from a pencil sharpener. I had managed to steal the scissors she had brought to school, but didn't think of the tiny blades in those cheap, harmlessly colourful bits of plastic.

I tried to follow her into the toilets, but I was met with odd looks and plenty of jeering from the football jocks.

'BURTO'S A GIRL!' they'd scream.

Their wit was so impressive that I would have had to pick myself up off the ground from laughing, but I had other things to worry about.

Simon and I could be found hanging around outside the girls' toilets at lunchtime, waiting for Mary to emerge. Her eyes would be red, her face tender and freshly washed from tears. I would make her laugh and we wouldn't talk about it. But despite my best efforts, it seemed there was nothing I could do.

I kept trying.

It was only a matter of time before Simon worked it out. And Mary got worse at hiding it. Her long-sleeved jumpers in the height of summer left her sweating and dizzy, but she refused to take them off. She seemed out of control and dark.

'You know I think you're amazing, right?' I'd offer when she was down.

Her face darkened with rage. 'You don't under-stand,' she'd say.

Why did giving her a compliment make her angry?

One afternoon we were perched on the sharp

embankment that looked out over the oval. Simon was practising for the upcoming athletics carnival. Mary and I had been silent for a long time.

'I wish you'd stop doing this to yourself,' I said, quietly.

Her face was pale. Her eyes didn't move. They were staring into empty space.

'You don't understand,' she said. 'It helps.'

'But it must hurt. It can't be good for you. I don't know why you'd do that to yourself.'

Nothing. Only more silence.

'You're hurting my best friend,' I said. 'And I don't like that. You're a good person. You're worthy of love and respect. Not pain.'

Her face hardened and she turned to me.

'David,' she said. 'Shut the fuck up.'

More than anything, I wanted to fix her. I attempted to understand the pain and dissect it. I took her suffering on as a personal mission. What sort of friend was I if I didn't? But nothing worked. I thought many times of asking for help, but this seemed like the ultimate betrayal. Mary had made me promise not to tell anyone, and I was terrified that if I let the secret out I would lose her forever. Simon was just as bewildered as I was, and the two of us were forced to sit and watch our friend unravel, with me trying to put the pieces back together like a mad man.

Going to school started to make me feel sick again. But this time I wasn't worried about my own health, I was worried about Mary's. I was certain I would show up one morning to a school assembly and the principal would take the stage and begin with something like, 'I'm afraid we have some very bad news...'

My own mood started to plummet. At home I was introverted, grumpy and prone to anxiety. But I was too worried about Mary to notice.

Mum and Dad, who were all too familiar with the mechanisms and symptoms of depression, began to suggest that I needed help. It wouldn't have been the first time I'd seen someone for black moods. But I insisted that I was fine. It became terribly important to me that I didn't accept help. I thought I needed to prove that I was functional and independent. At the time, my brothers' attempts to fit into their high school were causing a lot of stress, and Dad was in the middle of some professional woes. I was desperate not to be a burden; I wanted to be 'normal'. Just what that meant I was yet to figure out.

My appetite was almost non-existent. Mum began packing more extravagant and dessert-filled lunches, but my lunchbox would be returned each day, almost untouched.

'You need to eat,' she insisted. 'You need to see a doctor.'

After many months of Mum's repeated requests, I relented.

'I'll go and see a GP, but only if that's the end of it. I go and see him and then that's it.'

With no other choice, Mum agreed.

Our GP was an elderly and gentle man whom the family had seen for years. Mum booked an appointment for one day after school, and she escorted me into his dark office.

'So,' he asked me, 'what's the problem?'

I looked to Mum. I certainly wasn't going to elucidate. After all, I was 'fine'.

'Well,' Mum began with a sigh, 'he's not eating anything like he should be. He's anxious, and he has a lot going on at school. He's not sleeping. He's not communicating, and we're worried. I think he's depressed.'

The GP smiled, and looked to me.

'What grades are you getting in school?' he asked.

I shrugged. Grades had never been much of a problem for me. I told the truth.

'A's. The occasional B.'

The doctor looked at Mum.

'He's not depressed.'

I won.

My performance of 'fine' grew in boldness. Drama classes were my chance to let off steam. I'd approach each scene without fear, letting go and performing everything at ten times the normal size. I was the funny, crazy drama guy before, but now I was manic.

If anything, that was the version of me that seemed to help Mary the most. It made her laugh. I would count how many times she laughed during the day, attempting to track her mood. I kept a chart in the back of my maths book. Anything over a dozen was a good day. But it didn't seem to affect how much she cut herself.

The marks on her wrist got more savage. She could turn at any moment.

One day, she flew out of control. Simon and I were teasing each other, stealing each other's hats, and attempting to get Mary to join in. At first she was laughing, but when I took her hat she became red-hot with anger. She grabbed my hand, and pressed her nails into the skin of my arm. Tiny dots of blood appeared.

I dropped the hat in surprise.

'Ow!'

She snatched the hat from the ground and pushed it on her head.

'God, Mary,' Simon said. 'Lighten up.'

But Mary didn't say anything. Her face was wild

with fury and her eyes were suddenly shiny from tears. She stormed off in the direction of the toilets. After a few moments, Simon and I reluctantly followed her. She emerged from the toilets ten minutes later, her face clear and smiling.

'You okay?' I asked.

'Yeah,' she said. 'Why wouldn't I be?'

Before I had time to press her further, the bell rang for class. It was like nothing had happened. But the sleeves of her jumper were hooked around her fingers.

Not long after that, Simon and I were swapping notes on our crushes. I had moved on to another pretty girl, and Simon was way more interested in the opposite sex than he had been in the past. We were discussing how we should approach the recipients of our clumsy affection. Would they like us in return?

I turned to Mary. 'Who do you like?' I asked. It was the perpetual question at the heart of a lot of our gossip.

Mary looked at me.

'You,' she said.

The word echoed into a stunned silence.

Me.

Right.

I did what any proud male teenager does in the face of intense vulnerability.

I ran.

'Sorry, I've got to go prepare for my next class,' I said. And I physically ran away.

I was jarred by this news. I had honestly never considered it. The implications cascaded through my head. I thought about my conversation with her just before the revelation: I had been talking about a crush on another girl. Danielle. Or only last month, Christine! Actually, bugger that morning, that whole week, and the week before, the whole time...

I'd been talking about girls constantly, but never about her.

I began a very slow and delicate process of letting her down. Unfortunately, I was not exactly an expert at turning away love interests. I had never been attracted to Mary. As much as I wanted a relationship with someone, the idea of a relationship with her was frightening. What if, even then, I couldn't make her happy? I would surely be a failure of a boyfriend. I would make an even more awful boyfriend than I was a friend.

I pulled myself together and walked back to Mary. I apologised. 'I'm just a little surprised,' I said.

Mary nodded and looked down.

'I'm sorry,' I said again. 'I just think we should be friends, yeah?'

Nothing. Her hair was over her face.

'I'm sorry I talk about other girls. I didn't know how you felt.'

She nodded slowly.

And then I asked the question I already knew the answer to.

'Do you ever cut yourself because of me?'

Nothing.

And then she nodded.

I felt time slow down. I felt empty. Breathless. Floating.

The bell rang, and we went back to class.

We didn't talk about it.

That afternoon, I called Simon.

We both ended up in tears. The pressure had become too much. The two of us were fighting to keep this girl alive. I had failed at my mission. In trying to be kind, I had in fact made things worse. I was responsible for this awful situation.

'I told my parents about it,' Simon said.

'Yeah,' I sighed, 'I guess I should tell mine. It's just we swore we wouldn't.'

'I know, but we can't keep going like this.'

'What did they say?'

'They said we should tell someone at school. They want us to talk to the counsellor, or the principal.'

'No way! She'll never speak to us again. She'll kill herself,' I said.

Simon's voice sounded weak on the other end of the

phone. 'But Dave, she could kill herself anyway.'

Mum called me for dinner.

'I gotta go,' I said. 'I'll talk to you tomorrow and we'll figure it out then.'

We hung up.

The secret was starting to get out, and it was getting harder to find reasons to keep it hidden. No matter what Simon and I did, Mary was miserable.

That evening, after the twins had finished their spaghetti bolognese and left the table, I told Mum and Dad everything. They listened quietly. When I was done, Mum spoke. 'Simon's parents are right. The school should know. Mary's parents should know.'

I was terrified that this would happen. Mum had a track record for meddling, and the last thing we needed was her making a phone call to the school or to Mary's mum.

'No, Mum, please,' I pleaded. 'Please don't do anything. I'm serious. We don't know what she'll do.'

'It's not your responsibility, mate,' Dad said. 'You've done everything you can.'

'But no, please, don't call or do anything. Please. Just give me some time.'

Silence. Mum considered.

'Something's got to be done, David. She's in trouble. And it's not your responsibility to save her,' she said.

'But I'm her friend! And we made a promise not to tell anyone!'

I wasn't even really convincing myself anymore. I was so tired. Tired of making Mary Laughter Charts in my maths book. Tired of chasing after her. Simon, Mum and Dad were all saying the same thing: it was time to talk.

It felt like failure.

The next morning, without Mary knowing, Simon and I talked to a teacher, who then took us to the counsellor. The anonymous, placid woman listened to us with compassion.

'You are both good friends,' she said, 'and you've done the right thing. We'll take care of everything now, okay? There's nothing for you to do except keep being Mary's friend.'

I sighed. 'I doubt she'll be our friend after this.'

'Well, that's her decision. But she's lucky to have you both.'

We sat for a moment in silence. Simon and I were shell shocked.

The counsellor smiled. 'Okay? Time to go back to class, I think.'

Four minutes later we were back in English, studying a Shakespeare sonnet.

I guess, somehow, they did take care of everything, although I never figured out what happened after that. I assume they must have told Mary's mother, or got Mary in to talk. We never spoke to the counsellor again. It all felt so anti-climactic. Had Simon and I just betrayed our best friend? Or did we save her life? No one told us.

The next day, Simon and I approached Mary.

'Hi,' I said nervously.

She didn't look up from her book.

'I'm sorry, Mary. Can you tell us what happened?' Nothing.

'We just wanted to help you.'

It didn't matter what we said. Mary was no longer speaking to us. We kept trying throughout the day, but nothing happened.

According to Mary, we were gone.

Simon and I moved to sit with another group at lunch, and Mary disappeared at lunchtimes.

This was four weeks before the end of year ten. The only thing that stopped me from reaching back to her was my parents' calm insistence that I had to let her go and live her life. Her happiness was not my responsibility. I had done the right thing. I had told the truth.

Besides all of that, school and friends suddenly became fun again. Lunchtime was easy and stress free. I had forgotten what it was like to not have to worry intensely. But I felt guilty about not feeling more guilty.

Mary and I never spoke again. Mary left our high school at the end of that year and transferred to another school across town. I heard rumours of her putting on a New York accent and pretending to be a refugee from the 9/11 attacks. But that was the last I heard of her. I never saw her again.

When I think of Mary now, I think of our first playful interaction, her pale round face looking up at me, eyes warm, finger raised and pointing at my inky heart. She opens her mouth to speak, with genuine concern: 'Did you cut yourself?' she asks.

Sweet Sixteen

Right. I needed a shag.

I wish I could put into words the cataclysmic mix of hormones that is the infinite lust of a teenage boy. It's almost incomprehensible. I yearned to be an adult. I dreamed about my eighteenth birthday, where I'd suddenly have unlimited access to adult shops and pornography. When I was fully grown, I hypothesised, I'd be able to throw myself into all of these things without guilt. I'd have absolute freedom. I would wank for marathon sessions throughout each day. Now I find the thought of such things absolutely exhausting. I'd be such a disappointment to my teenage sexual self.

Actually, let's go back, to the very first time I learned about sex. When I was ten years old, my father sat me down to explain the facts of life. Slightly concerned by my increasing exposure to adult sitcoms (*Friends*, *Seinfeld*), he decided it was time to take me out for a manly chat. We sat on the front verandah, and he proceeded to give me a biology lesson. It was clinical, it was accurate, and it was essential. (It also, by the way, included the words 'some people are gay, which is fine'. Store that information for later on.)

Enthralled by my new knowledge about the human body, I proceeded to pass on the message to my best friends at the time: three sisters who were younger than me and who lived next door. The girls were bewildered by my new vocabulary. I impressed them with all kinds of new words, like 'sperm' and 'ovum' and, stirringly, 'urethra'. I walked away feeling very happy with myself. I was so damn smart. Those girls were lucky to have a friend like me.

When I told Dad that I had told the girls, he turned pale. He trudged next door to explain the situation. I don't know how the family reacted, but when Dad returned he had an urgent message for me. 'That type of information is special,' he said. 'People can feel very funny about that kind of thing.'

I found the secrecy perplexing. Dad couldn't explain to me why the family next door was afraid of this information, or afraid of what it could lead to. While Dad had given me an incredibly sound description of the process of sexual intercourse, he had left out two essential elements: sexual desire is incredibly powerful and sex is deeply pleasurable.

Over the next few years, I got the message loud and clear. We don't talk about sex, because sex is special. Those bullying kids in the playground who yell out 'dick' and the ones who kiss each other secretly are naughty and being silly. Sex is secret.

To assist with my adult education, Dad bought me a book (on my request). It was by one of my favourite authors at the time. *Secret Men's Business* by John Marsden was exactly what I needed. The book brilliantly answered a lot of questions about growing up male that I was too shy to ask, but it also mentioned a word I had never encountered before. Masturbation.

Like I did with all words I didn't know, I went to the dictionary and looked it up. I read the definition several times over, scarcely believing what I had read. My heart beat loudly in my chest.

This was an *option*?!

This is the story of how a young boy discovers himself, and how my high school years started. Ten hours before I put on my sparkling new Catholic high-school uniform and walked out the door to set upon a life that would lead me into adulthood, what did I do?

I masturbated. For the first time. Ever.

I remember the series of events with alarming clarity. I still had the dictionary in my hands when my Dad yelled out that there was time for me to take a bath before dinner. I went into the bathroom and undressed. I looked down at my penis. Somehow, in quite a short time and without my noticing, a *lot* of hair had grown around it, and it had almost doubled in size. It was one of the most bizarre experiences I've ever had: to look at my own body and see it in a whole new way.

I still didn't quite understand 'masturbation' as a concept. It seemed dirty. With that thought in mind, I looked underneath the bathroom sink and found two disposable latex gloves. I put them on and got in the bath, and I masturbated.

It was short, powerful and confusing.

I had not thought of the actual, um...end result of the whole process. So when it happened I was surprised. I was also immediately ashamed.

I felt absolutely awful.

Let's pause for a moment. How on earth did it come to pass that a perfectly normal and healthy teenage boy came to experience his body for the first time with a pair of latex gloves and several heaped tablespoons of shame?

It's hard to describe the primal level of self-disgust

I felt as I buried the latex gloves in the garbage in fear of one of my family members finding them. Without knowing it, I had caught the societal fear of sex that I had first encountered through the family next door.

It would not be until I was in my early twenties, a decade or more later, that I could ejaculate without feeling like I had dirtied myself. In my teenage years, I would make cold-hearted assertions that I would *not* touch myself anymore. But I'd inevitably be drawn back to it, thinking myself no better than a drug-addicted no-hoper each time.

I wasn't addicted; I was a teenager. I had enough hormones pumping through my body to resuscitate a small deceased horse. Masturbation feels good, it raises immunity, and it helps deal with stress.

My father had been amazing, doing more for me than many fathers do in teaching me about sex. The book he had given me was also incredibly advanced for its time. But neither of them had stopped what amounted to pretty ridiculous feelings of sexual shame.

Sex can be scary, and untamed teenage sexual desire can be dangerous and hurtful and lead to some pretty dark places. But repressing it doesn't do much good either. I certainly can't see any reason why I should have been afraid of or disgusted by my harmless pubescent willy and my innocent self-exploration.

For what it's worth, masturbation, as long as it's safe, private and you keep yourself well washed (no latex gloves needed), is completely normal. By the way, it can also help make you happy. But for me, as a teenager, there wasn't a single masturbation experience I could say I enjoyed. I wish I'd been told more emphatically that it was okay.

By year eleven, some four years later, things had become even more confusing. I had craved women, but that had ended in disaster; I had broken my best friend's heart and lost her as a result. I felt awful about the way I had left things.

So when it came to masturbation, I felt I was committing some awful sin. This wasn't helped by my fantasies, which were beginning to seem more like a hall of mirrors in my mind, shifting, changing and warping in a confusing fog.

Men started to show up. Naked, muscular, masculine fantasies began to run rampant. It was equal parts bewildering and alluring. Was I gay?

I desperately sought male affection and deep companionship. I found it nowhere. My friendship with Simon was a frustrating dead end. It was a relationship built on competition, never veering into emotional intimacy. We would argue about politics until we had shouted ourselves into exhaustion, but talking about our feelings was out of the question.

All my other friends were women, who were lovely, bright and wonderful, but I couldn't trust any of them with the contents of my sexual mind. It was a pity, because all I wanted to do was compare notes with someone: to see if they were as lost as I was. I had no idea if I was anywhere near normal. I had very little idea of what normal was. I couldn't escape the almost certain conclusion that no one was like me. All around me, my friends were dating, hooking up and dreaming of marriage and children. I had these dreams as well, but I also had an insatiable curiosity about the male body.

The question came again.

Am I gay?

I convinced myself that I wasn't. I was just curious. It was just my head playing tricks on me. I'd spend very quiet and shy hours looking up porn on the net (a more difficult task back in those days), and I watched men masturbating 'to see if I was doing it right'. I just wanted to know. With no one to talk to, porn became my only companion, one that I visited only in the dead of night and in desperate secret.

In the porn world, sex seemed to happen easily, and men were called upon to be aggressive, domineering and confident. I was none of those things. I found myself attracted to the more colourful range of men that could be seen in gay porn. It felt like I had a better chance of fitting in there. 'Bottom', 'top', 'twink', 'bear'—I was learning a new language for how to be a man.

The potential liberation that came with homosexuality was overshadowed by an anxiety that it meant I was a deviant. I didn't know anyone else who was gay and I assumed I would be outcast if I were to ever 'come out'. I was convinced my father would disown me and that my friends at school would ostracise me.

Plus, I wasn't repelled by women, and I still clung to a romantic idea of marriage and children, something I was in no hurry to give up. I just didn't have any idea how to link the romantic ideal of the man that populated sitcoms and movies with the sexually confident aggressive man that I saw in hetero porn.

All of this was happening inside my head. In reality, I was still yet to kiss someone, or even 'go out' with anybody. At sixteen, this was deeply unfashionable. By some bizarre accident, Simon had had a girlfriend for a few months now. I felt as though everybody was having sex but me. Couples seemed to spring up everywhere, and news of their sex status was updated frequently through the gossip circles. Some were holding off. Others were diving in. Some had said it would be a 'schoolies' thing. In my mind, everyone was shagging everywhere—a quickie beside the bunsen burners in chemistry, or a fondle underneath the desks in maths. Meanwhile, I was playing with my protractor and wondering what the hell was going on.

In retrospect, this was the greatest trick. We all played it on each other. I realise now that there was far less debauchery than any of us realised. We were incredibly celibate. The amount of actual sex was tiny compared to the amount of pretending we all did.

But I was determined to get a girlfriend, to prove to everyone, especially myself, that I was capable of being straight and sexually active. My crushes were about as constant as a revolving door, but at the beginning of year eleven, my heart belonged to Tiff. And I had somehow become sensitive enough to realise that her heart belonged to me.

Tiff had only been at the school for six months. Her enthusiasm for drama quickly made us companions in class, and her overall bubbly attitude was a salve after the troubles with Mary.

Tiff was a petite girl going through a goth phase. The strokes of eyeliner made her blue eyes all the brighter. Her jet black hair fell in loose bundles onto her shoulders. She was quiet. She wasn't looking to impress anyone. But she impressed me. I fell into the deepest infatuation I had known.

The group Simon and I sat with at lunch was now larger and more fluid. Rules about social structure were less intense than they had been when we were all starting out. Tiff was a part of this larger group, and we had become close enough friends to warrant our own outing.

By ourselves.

With each other.

With each other, by ourselves.

It looked, felt and smelt like a date, but we both vehemently denied it was one.

We went and saw *Chicago*.

Yep.

Chicago. The musical.

But I wasn't gay.

Tiff and I both loved musicals. We were enormous fans of *Moulin Rouge*, which had come out a few years earlier.

There was something about the bigness of it all that I liked. I was repressing so much of my true self, believing myself to be fundamentally unworthy of any kind of love. It was my belief that I was an awful friend and a generally awful person. These movies, in all their theatricality, provided a dizzyingly attractive freefall of emotional release. I suspect Tiff felt much the same. And in that darkened movie theatre, outside school and with a taste of freedom, we began a very quiet conversation.

'Is there anyone you like?' I asked. 'At school?'

She smiled slowly, and a light grew behind her eyes. 'Maybe. What about you?'

I concentrated on making sure my voice didn't break. 'Maybe,' I croaked. 'But what about you?'

'Maybe,' she replied, shyly. 'What about you?'

I giggled. 'Maybe.'

Silence for a while. And then I replied, 'What about you?'

She looked down. 'Maybe,' she said quietly. 'What about you?'

As gripping as this conversation was, I'll skip past its true length and get to the point.

'I might...like...you,' I said quietly.

I looked up.

She was smiling.

'You too,' she said.

We both laughed. I felt elated.

'Do you maybe want to go out with me?' I asked.

She giggled again, her eyes growing brighter.

'Yes.'

I'd won. I had a girlfriend. I'd done it. Finally. It was official. Tiff and I were going out. I was over the moon. Yes. Amazing.

Okay. Cool.

But now what?

With this quiet agreement of mutual attraction, I had expected something to kick in. I had expected my horniness to spin out of control. After all, didn't all teenage men want sex? And now that I was in a relationship, shouldn't I somehow be pursuing it pretty much relentlessly? I presumed the proud male aggression and confidence would just turn up once I was with someone.

But it didn't kick in. In fact, my libido plummeted. The thought of sex filled me with dread. I couldn't even kiss her. My entire body would tense up at the thought, and I would be incapable of speaking, let alone gallantly picking her up in my arms and depositing her softly onto a bed.

But we needed to kiss. And soon. The days were ticking past.

I was paralysed with fear. How is this meant to happen? What am I supposed to do? Do I just close my eyes and move in? Should I hold her head? But won't that be weird? Should I lick my lips? But won't that look friggin' creepy?

I had wanted a girlfriend for years. And Tiff was perfect in every way. You've got to listen to me on this point: there was nothing wrong with Tiff. Her startling blue eyes and gorgeous laugh made her wonderfully attractive, in every way. She was permanently energetic and full of humour. We made each other laugh. In her, I had found a kindred spirit. She felt somewhat out of place in her family and underestimated her own potential for greatness. I was drawn to her.

It was clear that *I* was supposed to initiate physical

affection. That was something that the guy was definitely supposed to do. When we said goodbye to each other at the end of the day, or found ourselves alone somewhere, she would look at me, expectantly, and there would be a silence that seemed to last an eternity.

'Okay,' I'd say. 'Bye.'

She'd give a half smile. 'See ya.'

We'd look into each other's eyes, and I would hear her brain telepathically screaming at my mine, demanding I take action. 'KISS ME.'

But I couldn't. I'd just nod and smile and leave.

I'd walk away feeling as though I'd failed a very important test. I couldn't bare to look back over my shoulder.

But Tiff kept giving me second chances. Each time, her face would shine up at me, full of optimism and hope for something I couldn't bring myself to deliver.

Friday came around. Our first week of being a couple had ended. I knew in my gut that *this* was a key time to make a move.

'I'll miss you this weekend,' I said. Her hand was tightly gripped in mine.

'Aw,' she said, looking down, embarrassed. And then I saw her have an urgent thought, and she lifted her face up to mine, so it was only inches away.

I felt as though I was about to collapse in a nervous puddle.

'I'll talk to you online?' I asked.

'Yeah,' she said, smiling.

Silence.

Long, horrible silence.

'Okay,' I said. 'I'll see you next week.'

'Okay,' she said.

Silence.

Again.

Longer, more horrible silence.

I walked away, trying to ignore the disappointment on Tiff's face.

Dammit.

I was beginning to question this whole relationship thing. Because nothing else had changed. Tiff and I cuddled, but we still acted like we were friends. Was being a boyfriend just being a friend, but with kissing?

The following Wednesday was Valentine's Day. I gave her a flower and a deluxe edition of *Moulin Rouge*.

Two weeks went by. In teenage-relationship time, that is close to a year. I hadn't done anything except hold her hand, cuddle her and buy her a gift. My lack of action was making our friendship, which was once so easy, awkward and weird. I felt like an idiot every time I opened my mouth. I couldn't begin to guess what she was thinking.

I attempted to talk to Simon about my confusion, but he was shocked at my complete lack of ability.

'Why don't you just do it?' he asked, exasperated.

'I don't know how.'

He shrugged. 'You just do it.'

'Yeah, but how though?'

'You're thinking about it too much. Just shut up and do it.'

Right. Good advice, Simon. Just do it.

Okay.

We had a drama excursion to Brisbane. The production was hilarious, but I found it difficult to enjoy. Tiff and I were at the back of the theatre, our hands tightly clasped, her head on my shoulder. It was Friday again, and I had two options. Kiss her now, or make a date to see her privately over the weekend, which meant one of us visiting the other, and the idea of attempting to pash with either of our families nearby was pure torture. So it had to be today. We couldn't go another whole weekend without something happening.

This was it.

On the bus ride back, Tiff's head kept finding its way to my shoulder, and her finger tickled the inside of my palm, drawing neat little circles. This new threshold of intimacy was too much. The bus was hot and my deep-fried lunch suddenly felt unsettled. I couldn't do this. When we arrived back at school, even the teacher gave me a wink and a nod. She had seen Tiff snuggling into me in the rear-view mirror. Oh God, everyone was about to find out I was a fraud.

Tiff was beaming, but I was internally screaming. This all felt so wrong and weird. I was bound to let her down. I would inevitably be shit. In place of lust, I felt crippling fear.

She looked up at me, smiling, saying goodbye. We had waited until the school courtyard was deserted, my stomach tightening all the while. We held hands and looked at each other, and the heavy, familiar silence opened up between us, the dim echo of my own failings reverberating between us.

She was waiting.

'Bye,' I said, and walked away.

Just as I had suspected I would, I completely buggered up. I was an awful boyfriend. I couldn't even kiss her.

On Monday, Simon advised me to break it off.

So I did. I convinced myself that she must have been feeling very similar to me.

'I just feel like we're better off going back to the way we were,' I said, trying not to look her in the eye. 'I think we're meant to be friends.'

Tiff gave a short, silent nod. And then she smiled.

We hugged.

It was over.

I felt instantly relieved. Now I didn't have that to worry about. I breathed easy. I went back to being funny Crazy Drama Dave, and Tiff and I went back to being friends. I convinced myself she was fine, probably just as relieved as I was.

'It's great,' I said to Simon one day. 'I don't know why we tried to be anything more. She thinks so too.'

Simon was not convinced. 'She's devastated. I don't think you realise. She's really upset.'

I shrugged it off. What did he know? I ignored any sense of failure, and just put my first dating experience down as an experiment that didn't pay off. There'd be someone else soon enough.

A week later, I noticed marks on Tiff's wrists.

6

Yoo-hoo!

My internal wrestle with love and lust was the tip of the iceberg in a time that would see my entire year level go mental. We were fast approaching the final year of school, and the pressure was on. Relationships were secured and broken up in a matter of days. Virginities were willingly given and taken. Alcohol-fuelled parties, I heard (although I never attended them), were abundant. But our blossoming sexuality was only one part of senior high school. Chaos abounded everywhere. There were rumours of other girls self-harming, and two or three students came to school with dark bruises and tales of family fights gone horribly wrong.

School itself didn't help. Assignments grew in length and ferocity, piling one on top of the other. Relentless pep talks about responsibility and becoming an adult only served to raise anxiety levels. We were asked, almost daily, what we intended to do when we left school. And we weren't even in our final year. It seemed that every second week we were drawing up a list of goals, either spiritual, academic or personal. Adults made every effort to instil in us a spirit of aspiration. But this rarely had the desired affect of turning our attention outward and to the sky, inspired by the prospect of a bright and sparkly future. More often it left us feeling as though being the natural people that we were just wasn't good enough. We had to get better marks, achieve greater successes and create more unique opportunities before we could be fit to join society. Left to just be ourselves, we were significantly less than ideal.

Wonderfully, my parents exerted next to no academic pressure on me, a piece of good fortune that didn't befall the majority of my peers. My folks probably picked up that I was manufacturing more than enough anxiety all by myself. I had no idea what I wanted to do with my future, and I was almost certain my career choices would be limited by my perverse sexual desires and the fact that I could barely walk past a female without somehow making her suicidal.

Drama classes, my one forum of unrestrained

expression, changed significantly in senior years. Mrs Coates, whose altar I had knelt at and who had inspired so much confidence, left the school to become a parent. The drama teachers who remained were equally competent, but nothing could persuade me from my singular devotion to the now-absent Mrs Coates.

She left me with a parting gift, however. Her husband was a drama teacher at an all-boys school across town, and I received a phone call inviting me to participate in their weekly drama group after school. I would be the only boy in attendance who was not enrolled in the school. No girls were allowed.

I had thought my own co-ed school was about as chaotic as any school could get. I knew nothing.

I arrived at the empty unknown music hall on a frosty Thursday night, not daring to think of what lay ahead. Inside the hall (which was wonderfully better resourced than my own school) were a couple of dozen rowdy teenage boys, playing a game that seemed to be made up of a lot of tagging, tackling and yelling. I spied the friendly familiar face of Mr Coates across the hall, and he approached.

'Hi, mate,' he said. 'Just join—'

But he was interrupted by a shout across the room. 'FUCK OFF, LIAM!'

Mr Coates raised his eyebrows. 'Callum,' he said, warning.

'Sir, Liam pulled my pants down.'

It was true. Callum was pulling his pants up from around his ankles. The offender, Liam, was in hysterics. Mr Coates smiled and turned back to me.

I was shocked. At my school, a dacking or swearing would easily land you in detention. Here, Mr Coates had done little but raise his eyebrows. The whole thing had played out with smiles. Everyone enjoyed the joke, even Callum, who had had his blue underwear shown to everyone. It was a different world.

'Join in,' said Mr Coates. 'We'll get started soon.'

I entered into the fray. 'Guys,' yelled out Mr Coates. 'This is Dave. He'll be joining us tonight.'

I received a few nods of recognition, and play resumed. That was it. I was welcomed. The game had now evolved into tackle, tag and dack. Pants were flying up and down quicker than could be seen.

I had entered a super-charged masculine circus. Compared to the restrained and almost entirely female drama class at my school, the boys' drama club was like a late-night cable special.

When the evening began proper, we launched into a series of improvised scenes that seemed to have no rules. The social communication was a battle of wits; we were competing for the dirtiest jokes and the most creative and liberal use of profanity. Silliness was embraced. Nonsense was applauded. Friendships were made quickly and easily, and any initial fears I had about being an outsider dissolved in the thunderous cloud of Pythonesque madness.

I went every week, and considered the boys my friends, even though we shared little beyond the funny scenes. We never swapped secrets or had anything more than giggly conversations, but an intimate camaraderie grew out of the club's ambitious performance schedule, which saw us delivering a new bare-bones production every couple of months.

The shows were spectacles in themselves: equal parts classic comedy sketches, original stories and utter chaos. The audience, of parents and friends, was treated to students fire-breathing in intermission. Hastily thrown-together bands would play. Backstage was a mess of props and piles of unlearned scripts, and it smelled straight-up of sweaty balls.

I had some of the best nights of my life there. Away from the politics of school, I allowed myself to be the loud and expressive drama kid without limits, and I was surrounded by peers who embraced the opportunity in exactly the same way. I slowly began to realise that the boys were the outcasts of their school, and the club was an important refuge for them too from the sport-saturated environment of their day-to-day school life.

The real success of the performance evenings were the original pieces written by Mr Coates. Presented as an episodic adventure, these shows focused on a boy and his gang of imaginary friends, with recurring characters. So each of us was given a character that we would improvise and slowly build over time.

'Okay,' began Mr Coates one evening, 'we need to write the next show. Tonight we'll come up with some new characters. You'll get a piece of paper with a name and a few words of description, and then we'll start playing around.'

The hat was passed around. I pulled out a piece of paper.

'Eugene,' it read. 'Hare-brained professor.'

We got up in small groups to introduce ourselves. One of the central rules of improvisation is that you don't think. You just *do*. So when Eugene introduced himself I was just as surprised as anyone else was.

'Helllloooooo!' came Eugene's effeminate drawl. 'I'm Professor Eugene, and I'm here to conduct *experiments*.'

I arched my eyebrows on the final line, and dropped my hands to circle my nipples, slowly. The boys erupted into laughter.

Just like that, Eugene was born.

Without meaning to, I had created a gigantic caricature of the type of man I was terrified of becoming. He was a big, flaming fag. An emphatically effeminate, limp-wristed, barely-closeted homosexual.

His jokes were not based on wit, but on thinly-veiled attempts to crack on to the other boys with ceaseless innuendo (in-your-end-o). He would return for every show. He would say things the other boys would not say, perhaps because I didn't have to attend the school the following day.

'I hear a noise!' Eugene said, in a memorable haunted-house outing. 'I feel energy...wait, I can feel it...'

At this point Eugene closed his eyes and let his hands wander, attempting to feel 'energy'. 'I'm getting a strong, pulsating kind of vibe. It's coming from... right here!'

I'd open my eyes, right on cue, I was pointing right at one of the other boy's genitals. The teenage audience applauded; the joke was pure scandal.

In another show, Eugene described his recipe for a meaty bolognese. 'Lots of meat and plenty of cumin.' (Pronounced, of course, as come-in.) 'I love *CUM-in*.'

Hard to believe this original wit didn't instantly launch a national comedy career.

Still, our audiences grew, and the characters became known and attracted their own followings. Soon, my classmates started attending performances, interested in how I was spending my Thursday nights. I so enjoyed the bountiful audience laughter with every limp-wristed 'Yoo-hoo!' that Eugene yelled out into the crowd. I was terrified of being gay, but Eugene absolutely loved it, and his audience loved it too.

On stage my most private of fears were brought out in freakish exaggeration, and the result was adolescent comedy gold. It was terrifying and thrilling. I left each night feeling free and light, as if I had shed some intense weight.

My performances in every regard were accomplished for my age. The advice I had given to Mary— 'just don't be yourself'—had evolved for me into a constant and extroverted piece of fraud. No one knew of my anxiety. No one.

In fact, I had become a leader at school. I was loud, sarcastic and running so fast my feet barely touched the ground. I was in the choir, two school bands, the school production, debating, mooting, and on any committee that would have me. In year twelve, the young man who had started school by being thrown across a visual arts table was voted School Vice Captain.

I didn't tell anyone how I actually felt. I was constantly anxious and depressed underneath an extroverted guise. I was putting an extraordinary amount of work into being a liar, and for the trouble I was elected as a school leader and promoted as a role model to my peers. In every way, my deception was rewarded.

It was only a matter of time before it all fell apart.

Bruises

I didn't comment on Tiff's wrists. No one did. Besides, year eleven was nearly over. I made the final sprint through exams and collapsed into my summer holidays. I was exhausted. It was hard to believe that in just twelve months I would be graduating from high school. The thought was too scary to contemplate. Anyway, I had to survive year twelve first.

The difference between year eleven and year twelve was palpable. We all felt it the moment we walked through the door on our first day back. Our teachers reminded us constantly that we were no longer students, we were 'leaders'. My extra-curricula activities doubled as I took on as many responsibilities as my Vice School Captain status could allow.

Simon was still by my side, and our friendship group was stable. The summer holidays had provided a convenient break for Tiff and me, and we resumed being friends as if nothing had happened.

In that final year of intense academic pressure, you may be surprised to learn that my friends and I didn't talk that much about exams, or the concept of leadership, or our future as adults (or, as our teachers insisted upon calling it, our 'sacred journey'). We didn't ruminate on Catherine's inner-motivation in *Wuthering Heights*, which we studied for English. We didn't interrogate the quadratic equations that we were studying in maths.

We mostly talked about the formal.

There are three critical ingredients required for a formal: dancing skill, formal wear and a partner.

For one afternoon a week leading up to the formal, the entire senior school body would pile into our massive gymnasium and learn dances that we would NEVER DANCE AGAIN, except at our own children's formals, perhaps. Nevertheless, we threw ourselves into the task as if we were living in a Jane Austen novel and this was the only way we would ever fit into society.

The dances all had archaic names that seemed to encourage us to go back to a simpler time when women were subjugated and gender lines were crystal clear. The 'Merry Widow Waltz', the 'Marching through Georgia', and my favourite, the 'Pride of Erin'. Who the hell was Erin? And why was I displaying my pride through dance?

We learnt the dances in two giant circles: the men on the outside, the women on the inside, and we swapped partners every few bars or so. As each girl arrived in my arms, they inevitably said, 'God, you're so much better than the other guys at this.'

I cursed God. Yes, apparently I had rhythm.

An alarm went off in my brain.

GAY GAY GAY.

I attempted to cover up my dancing prowess by constantly mucking up the moves. That the world has missed out on my natural dancing abilities is something many people are weeping over to this day. (Don't worry. Upon request, I can break into the Pride of Erin with a moment's notice.)

The second ingredient proved to be slightly trickier than the first. I wish I could say I pondered extensively what type of suit to wear, but I didn't. I knew exactly what I wanted months in advance.

In the shop window of a quiet menswear store were three matching zoot suits. One in garish yellow, another in lime green, and another in royal purple. I decided I wanted the purple one. I would go to my senior formal in a purple suit.

Let me try to explain why I wanted to look like a Batman villain.

To wear a black suit, or anything resembling what most of the men were wearing, felt like a betrayal of who I was. It would be a lie to say I was a normal man, because I wasn't. The purple suit fitted perfectly with my extroverted, clownish, Eugene-like persona. Not only that, it had a bright yellow silk lining and shirt, a glaring purple tie and two-tone purple-and-gold shoes. As ridiculous as it was, it was the perfect suit for me. I was the perfect joke of a man.

Problem was, the suit in the shop window was expensive. I was insistent that that was what I wanted, and my mother was sympathetic. But we couldn't afford it. Mum, however, had the skills to make a replica from scratch.

So, months away from the big day, Mum bought a pattern and started making a purple zoot suit tailored for my skinny teenage frame. After all, she didn't have enough to worry about with my two disabled brothers battling high school (we will return to them later).

The third element, finding a partner, was a complicated social dance in itself. The entire year level tricked each other into believing that couplings were arbitrary, and usually based on casual companionship as opposed to romantic desire. But the opportunity served as a chance for those harbouring long-time crushes to try their luck. All around me, new dating partnerships emerged.

Since Tiff and I had broken up, I had all but given up on finding a partner. Despite being constantly drawn to naked men in my mind, I was equally attracted to finding a wife and living a beautifully quiet, normal life. In fact, I believed it would be my salvation. I believed in my romantic vision. I would be a normal man, and find someone who would accept me.

I had plenty of crushes, but I found it difficult to take the next step and actually do something about it. This is true for most guys. But for most guys, it's a fear of rejection. I was stopped by a fear of success. What would happen if a girl said yes, and suddenly I was in a Tiff situation again? I would stuff it up and destroy the poor girl's heart. I felt as though I should come with a warning sign around my neck: 'Loving me will almost certainly result in wrist-cutting.'

I needed a risk-free partner.

Because we were friends, and because I felt comfortable with her, and because I knew I couldn't let her down more than I already had, I asked Tiff. She said yes. Simple. Easy. No stress. The marks on her wrist had faded, and our friendship had resumed its natural course.

It would all be fine.

Right?

I watched with interest as a blonde girl named Maddie began a campaign to take a female partner to the formal. The year was 2004, and teenage homosexuality was really only a shadow on the public consciousness. Maddie ended up getting her way. She was the first open lesbian in the school's history. The students didn't really care. But it was a long debate between Maddie and the staff, who at first dismissed her desires as a cry for attention. She went to the formal with her girlfriend. If it was a cry for attention, it was one of the bravest cries I'd ever witnessed.

Maddie was tolerated, but not accepted. I had the opportunity to get involved in the debate as a representative of the student body, almost all of whom didn't care who Maddie took to the formal beyond making it a subject of rumours. But the thought of actually using my School Vice Captain status to help Maddie's campaign for acceptance never crossed my mind. Instead, I took part in the schoolyard rumours as the saga played out. It was such a delicious scandal. Looking back, I can't imagine what Maddie was actually going through.

Also becoming prone to gossip was the boys' drama group I was part of across town. With our audiences growing, we were determined to push the envelope on what was acceptable, and every show was immediately followed by a long list of complaints from the principal. We enjoyed getting in trouble. I had no concerns at all, as I didn't attend the school and I didn't have to put up with the principal's disciplinary lectures.

But it was only a matter of time before things went too far. A week before the formal, a showcase evening turned to near tragedy when a fire-breathing routine got out of hand. An inexperienced young man swallowed the fire accelerant. He believed that fire breathing meant you breathed the fumes of fuel to make the fire whip into fantastical shapes. In fact, fire breathing is spitting very small quantities of fuel onto lit torches, followed by intensive mouth-rinsing immediately afterwards. It shouldn't be attempted by anyone who hasn't had extensive training in performing the stunt.

The victim of stupidity and poor supervision was rushed to hospital to get his stomach pumped, and the drama club became the focus of concerned parents and teachers. The principal had to fight off cancelling it altogether. Fire breathing was banned.

I was disappointed, but my mother took it further. The day before the formal she put her foot down and said I wasn't to attend anymore.

I was horrified.

'Mum! No way! It's the best part of the week for me!'

'I don't care,' she said. 'You're not going. I don't trust Mr Coates. It's dangerous and irresponsible.'

'You can't do this. I'll go anyway.'

'Then you'll walk.'

I was furious.

'Fine.'

Mum had a lot going on at the time. Her depression now manifested as acute stress migraines, and her nights were often interrupted by visits to hospital for injections to relax her muscles. I woke up regularly to red beams of light flashing through my bedroom windows. Mum would call an ambulance and attend the hospital alone, asking them not to turn the siren on so they wouldn't wake the rest of the family.

Teenagers aren't particularly sensitive beasts, and so I didn't take any of this into account when I threw a petulant adolescent tantrum, stating repeatedly that I would be going to the drama club with or without her permission. Our argument escalated.

'I cannot believe you're doing this to me,' I said, growing in anger.

'David, it's not safe.'

'It's like you *want* to make me miserable.'

Down the hall, on a coathanger, was the purple suit that Mum had now been stressing over for months. It had all the markings of a zoot suit: a silk lining, interior pockets, a pleated waist band. It was a work of art. I had said thank you on a number of occasions, but now Mum was saying that I wasn't nearly as grateful as I should be. Soon we weren't talking about fire breathing at all, but about how she, somehow, in my teenage mind, didn't understand or support me. I declared that she never supported me.

'If this were the twins asking,' I said, 'you wouldn't have a problem.'

Her eyes flew wide open with tears and anger.

Dad said, quietly, from his corner, 'I think that's enough now.'

Mum started yelling at me. Really yelling. Properly yelling. I had never heard her voice so high and vicious before. I remember her eyes: wild, bloodshot eyes that burned out at me from a body rigid with fury. She got up and stormed out of the house. She slammed the car door, backed out of the driveway at a God-awful speed and raced down our street.

This had never happened before. Our family's first defence was to avoid conflict. In a choice between confrontation and silence, we chose silence every time at all costs. No one in the family had ever argued the way Mum and I just had. Certainly, no one had ever stormed out of the house and straight-up left.

Dad and I were suddenly alone, stunned. Our first concern was the boys who were in their bedroom. They must have heard the yelling. If they knew that Mum had left in a distraught state, they would likely have an anxiety attack that would need a significant boost of meds to calm them down. Dad and I went in and assured them everything was fine. They nodded their understanding with complete and oblivious trust.

It was a strange afternoon, waiting for Mum to come back, worried that she might never return. Dad and I went back to our routines without talking. He went to the computer; I went to my room.

What had just happened? And what was going to happen? Would Mum come back?

We didn't have to wait too long. I was in my room when I heard the car pull in and Mum storm out. She opened the front door to find Dad.

'I'm packing my bags and going!' she yelled.

'I think you need to calm down, love,' Dad said.

'Don't PATRONISE ME!'

I knew Mum was headed for me. She was sure to come to my room. I had to hide. More than that, I had to get to the boys. What would they do if they saw Mum in this state? What would Mum do? I quickly ran the long way to the boys' bedroom, hiding from the escalating argument between Mum and Dad.

I raced in and closed the door. The boys were sitting in their second-hand lounge chairs, staring mildly at the television. They looked up at me calmly.

'What's wrong?' Andy asked.

'Nothing,' I smiled. 'Nothing.'

I heard movement in the lounge room, Mum screaming.

'What's that?' Chrissy asked.

'Let's put some music on.' I went to the CD player and turned up the music. A plastic pop tune blared out from the speakers. The boys and I danced and sang wildly; all the while my heart was pounding in my chest. We could no longer hear what was going on outside.

I felt a part of me break. The boys were happy and beautifully ignorant, but I went a little nuts, singing and dancing with them. Pretending everything was fine while the world was ending outside. Pretending, for a moment, that I was some kind of protective brother, or a good son.

The song ended, and there was no noise.

Silence.

Safety.

Right. I should get back to my bedroom. If Mum comes in to confront me in front of the boys...

I make a quick duck to my room and close the door. I don't run into Mum. I think she's up the hallway, in her own bedroom. I wait, breathing heavily by the door. I'm scared. I've never been scared of Mum before. It's never been like this.

I hear her stomping up the hallway and then the terrible pounding of her knock. She swings the door open and I jump over the bed, out of the way, away from her.

I'm sure she's going to hit me. I'm almost positive it's going to happen. My mind races to those kids at school with their dark bruises. I tell her, I scream at her through tears that I'm sorry. I'm sorry for what I said. I was angry and I was stupid.

She stares at me with cold, wild eyes. She's not my mum. I don't recognise her. She's not my mum. She opens her mouth to speak. There are tears in her eyes. The sharp shrill of anger has disappeared, and it's replaced by a deeply certain and guttural tone.

'You're a horrible, awful son. You're ungrateful and you do nothing for this family.'

She turned around and left, slamming the door behind her.

I punch myself repeatedly in the head as I cry.

It's about 5pm, and I don't leave my room until the following morning to go to school.

My mum is there, like she always is. We don't speak of the events the previous evening. Everything is normal.

That night, I put on my purple suit. Tiff comes to my front door. Her parents are driving us in their vintage car. I give her a corsage and she gives me a peck on the cheek. We pull off a seamless performance in front of our parents. Her dress is dark blue. I take her by the arm. Side by side like this, we look like a bruise.

Everyone laughs at my suit, and I laugh with them. I am funny and energetic. I mimic joy perfectly. I am expected to dance with my mother for a song or two. I take her by the hand and lead her round the floor. Other mothers have tears in their eyes. We are awkwardly stilted, false.

Then I danced with Tiff. I was in a gigantic purple suit, playing a madman, dancing with my ex-girlfriend who I'd let down and my mother who hated me. This was so stupid. I was so stupid. I'd never felt more like a fraud.

∿∿∿

I kept expecting another conversation between my mother and me, but it never came. School and family life moved on. My Crazy Drama Dave performance continued at breakneck pace.

Then, a month before school was scheduled to finish, in the middle of my final exams, I woke up to a startling realisation. It sunk into me like a freezing cold wave.

If I got out of bed, I would die.

I was paralysed from head to toe.

8

Doctors and Depression

Of course, this had been coming for a while. It had only been a matter of time before I went into a full-on meltdown.

Crazy Drama Dave had not fooled my parents all these years. I had been a different version of myself at home. I arrived at the end of every school day completely drained and exhausted, and retreated to my room for hours on end to watch meaningless television. I had little motivation to do or say anything when I was in this state of mind; I would usually only get up when I was called to dinner. I'd sit silent at the table, have a couple of mouthfuls, mumble that I wasn't hungry and return to my room.

After the GP visit back in the Mary days, Mum repeatedly tried to get me to go and see someone. But I wasn't budging.

'I'm fine,' I would insist, even fooling myself. I thought this was how I worked, normally. I certainly wouldn't have said I was happy, but then I didn't think happiness was even possible.

Besides, it wasn't like I didn't have experience with psychologists. In fact, I'd seen a handful of doctors before I'd gone anywhere near high school.

∿∿∿

'You know, it's okay to be depressed,' she says, gripping my knee and looking into my eye. The young psychologist is pretty. Her hair is tied back in a ponytail; her clothes are inoffensive and sensible. She exudes good intentions. The office is an altar to the idea of sound mental health: it's all warm inviting reds, couches of brown academic leather, cartographic art on the walls. (I've been to a lot of psychologists in my time; I don't know why they're obsessed with hanging old maps on the walls. Are psychologists ye olde sailors in their leisure hours? Do they know there are new ones available? I imagine them lost in suburbia, yelling into an olde scroll: 'Which way is north, Goddamit? *North?!*')

I'm ten at this stage, by the way.

'You shouldn't feel bad about feeling sad,' she continues.

It sounds like she's about to break into song.

'That rhymed,' I say, smiling. She returns the smile, but I detect pity. It's slight and small, with a gentle nod.

'It's okay to feel depressed,' she repeats. 'I mean, David, you've got a lot going on for a ten year old, don't you? Two brothers with Aspergers, you're picked on at school, you've got no friends, both your parents are on antidepressant meds so, you know. It's okay to be depressed.'

'Um...thanks?' I reply, uncertain. I wait for her to add to the list: 'You're pretty shit at sport too, and soon you'll have to go to high school, which will be a nightmare, and you don't know if God exists and what the purpose of life is and—OH, GOD!!' She bursts into tears and leaps out of the window, the glass shattering as she falls and kills herself on the bitumen below. I calmly exit the office and tell the receptionist that my psychologist has killed herself, and I look at my mum in the waiting room as if to say: 'See? I told you something like this would happen.'

But that doesn't happen. And I'm being unfair to this particularly nice woman. She's just trying to let me know that I have permission to feel sad. Even at this age, I've somehow picked up that it's less trouble if I just say 'I'm fine' when someone asks how I am. My stubborn denial of my real feelings has led me to this room. I'm not fine. There are lots of reasons I shouldn't be fine.

Sadness is one thing. Depression is something else. I have clinical depression. I know this because another psychologist told me a couple of years ago, when I was seven.

I was in grade three. I was experiencing anxiety that normal seven year olds weren't experiencing. I was outright paranoid.

Whenever Mum and Dad would leave me in a car even for just two minutes, I was certain something awful would happen to them. I'd imagine them being kidnapped or murdered, and even their safe return wouldn't convince me that they were safe. I was certain that impostors had killed my real parents and were adopting their skin as a disguise. I can't remember voicing these fears, as I was never sure that my parents were my *real* parents. I would occasionally accuse them of trying to poison me—a tantrum that my parents put down to exhaustion.

If I made the mistake of watching the news, I would instantly believe that my family was destined for whatever sorry fate the television exposed—nuclear disaster, fire, murder and robbery were the most common fears. I barely slept.

So Mum and Dad took me to a psychologist who

talked to me about 'stress'. 'Stress' was a new word in my vocabulary, and in my seven-year-old mind it was something that made me special. The following week at show and tell, I got up in front of the class, explained what stress was, and how I have it sometimes, and I even talked through some of the tools the psychologist had given me to relieve it. My seven-year-old peers seemed indifferent. I remember the smile on the teacher's face. It was the same as the one the psychologist would give me a few years later, when I pointed out that she was accidentally rhyming. It was a smile that said: 'I don't know what to do with this information. Who the fuck is this kid? Is this inappropriate?'

I'd learnt something new about myself and I wanted to share it. I didn't understand that you weren't supposed to get up in front of your class and talk about your mental-health difficulties. I got a sense of it that day though. No one said anything to me.

The psychologist who diagnosed me with stress was one of the very first psychologists my parents sent me to. His name was Lachlan. I was seven. I worshipped him. A person who would sit and listen to me...for a WHOLE hour?! He would sit and ask me questions and WANT to listen to my answers. Amazing.

The conversations with Lachlan quickly uncovered my incredibly low self-esteem. I was the victim of ongoing bullying at school, and I had begun to believe that the world was punishing me for being worthless.

Wisely, Lachlan and my parents were a little wary about giving a kid with anxiety and a case of the blues any mind-altering drugs. They sought different strategies. Lachlan gave me an exercise book. This was to be my 'positive thinking' book. Affirmations and lists of stuff I'd done successfully were to be written down in this book.

The only thing I really remember about the book was its cover. I'd wrapped it in bright red paper and stuck a picture of Genie from the Disney film *Aladdin* on the front alongside a picture of Robin Williams in *Good Will Hunting*. I admired Williams' artistry. He could play extroverted, joyful and silly, but also sombre, understated and lonely. I can't remember what I wrote in the book, and I don't know if it worked. But there must have been some kind of effect, because I didn't need to go back to Lachlan for a while.

I was an easy target at school: I was crap at sport, and I was regularly mistaken for a foreigner. I had dark skin and a surprising abundance of hair for a pre-pubescent. A lot of the class insisted that I must be from England. My family had been Australian for a handful of generations.

'But you talk like a Pom!' they'd say with disdain. I was speaking English. They were speaking an exotic dialect known as 'Bogan shithead'.

According to them (and, eventually, to myself), I was a girl. Gay. I wore the wrong things. I said the wrong things. I was just wrong.

My insomnia mutated into a significant problem. For about eighteen months I survived on very little sleep. As a nightly ritual, I'd go to the kitchen at around midnight, having attempted sleep for a few hours, cry for half an hour, and go back to bed. It went on for months. Mum and Dad tried every strategy under the sun. Some nights Mum would come out and make some toast, or give me special chocolates that she'd kept hidden. Other times she and Dad would ignore it, not speak of it, trying to deny my cry for attention. It may have been a cry for attention. I don't know what it was. Mum and Dad tried everything.

Constantly distraught over the bullying, Mum, Dad and I decided on a motto: 'What do I care what other people think?' I recited this to myself, over and over, during class taunts and when I was shoved into the sand in the playground. It helped. I was proud of it. It was my own little 'positive thinking' lesson.

We went back to Lachlan. I explained my mantra.

'Yeah,' he said. 'Good. But is that a short-term or long-term strategy? Is that going to work for a long time?'

'Oh,' I said, instantly deflated. Mum was furious.

Our little home-made exercise for sanity and self-esteem had been shot down. We didn't go back to Lachlan after that.

To be honest, I lose track of the psychologists after Lachlan. Eventually I gave up, and adolescent stubbornness took over. I would not go to a doctor. After all, I was *fine*.

Mum nagged at me about it for years. Days would pass without me eating, hours without speaking, many nights without sleep. When Mum finally got me to go to our GP, who provided the diagnosis 'he's not depressed' within two minutes of seeing me, I used it as a defence for years.

By the time I reached senior high school, I had come to see going to a psychologist or a doctor as a personal failure. Being an independent and accomplished man meant standing tall without help. Feeling anxious, stressed, or uncontrollably sad was an effeminate failing. There was little I could do about my gangly body, which was my inescapable evidence of physical weakness. My mind, however, was easier to disguise. Every day as I showered, brushed my teeth, and walked out the door without breakfast, I put on the mask of a confident young man. Inside, though, I was only making things worse by repressing my true feelings.

It's easy to underestimate the power of personal denial, but I had convinced myself that I was absolutely fine. I believed that I was as happy as I could be.

Thinking otherwise was absolutely terrifying. Even entertaining the idea that I needed help meant also accepting the possibility that I was gay, a bad friend, a terrible boyfriend, incapable of leading or responsibility, a burden on my parents, a negative influence on my brothers, and, therefore, a fundamentally unworthy human being.

But it was a fight I was always going to lose. The negative thoughts festered and grew wild, manifesting in all kinds of ways that I didn't expect. My immune system also suffered. It took me longer to bounce back from any minor illness. I was exhausted, sick and empty.

The result of years of denial was paralysing fear, and the inability to get out of bed. And it was just weeks before I was to finish high school.

Getting Out of Bed

I lay in bed and looked up at the ceiling.

A part of my brain spoke to me with grave certainty.

'If you leave this bed, you will die.'

My entire body felt heavy, as though it was sinking into the bed. I could hear sounds of morning: Mum battering away on the sewing machine, birds twittering outside, the soft mumble of television news. The world was completely normal, but inside my brain something had happened, telling me that today was dangerous. Potentially lethal. And I simply didn't have the strength to get up.

But there was another part of my brain that knew

this was ridiculous. This part was telling me that I was weak and idiotic, and over-dramatic. I needed to get up, have a shower and go to school. I was stronger than this.

I made my way to the bathroom in a light run, hoping my brain wouldn't catch up to what my body was doing. I looked up into the hot water, letting it cascade over my face but, rather than relaxing me, the water felt like needles piercing my skin. My chest began to feel tight and I couldn't take in a breath. The shower seemed to be getting smaller; the walls were closing in around me and distorting. The square tiles became circular. The drain seemed an eternity away. I thought I was going to die.

I didn't know it, but I was experiencing a panic attack. The core of it passed within a minute, but it left me instantly exhausted. As I stepped out of the shower and began to dry myself, most of my mental noise left me. It was replaced with a feeling of despair that was immovable. It had the weight of lead, as though every atom of my body was dragging downwards. I had a deep desire to bury myself in the earth, to feel the comfortable warm weight of soil pressed on my body, and be surrounded by nothing but absolute, dense silence.

Simultaneously, I felt empty. I didn't feel sad, or anxious, and certainly not happy or light. I felt as though I was incapable of any emotion, as though the energy required to crack a smile would also crack my heart, and I would lie down and die.

I told my parents that I wasn't going to school, and I went back to bed. I couldn't fight anymore.

∿∿∿

For the fortnight that followed, I spent most of my time in the bedroom. The main thing that surfaced in my mind was the matter of my sexuality—my unending confusion over my fascination with men.

I didn't see bisexuality as an option. I believed that I would be perceived as even more perverted if I was bisexual than if I came out as gay. I replayed every conversation I'd ever had with everyone I loved, to see if I could figure out how they would react to my coming out. I was sure they would all leave me, especially Simon, who had frequently expressed how uncomfortable he was with gay people and how they 'rubbed it in people's faces'.

At that time, the cultural language around homosexuality was only just becoming mainstream. I didn't have Kurt from *Glee*. Ellen DeGeneres was still several years from building her talk show. In 2004, my main sources of information about how gay people might go about their lives came from *Queer Eye for the Straight Guy* and *Will & Grace*. Both shows boasted flamboyant gay characters.

Was this the type of man I was destined to become? Would it be necessary to display my sexuality as the cornerstone of my personality? I was rubbish at cooking, found it incredibly difficult to tame my pubescent facial hair, and my one foray into fashion had been my purple zoot suit. This was evidence that I was a rubbish gay person. I feared that I would be rejected from the homosexual community for not fitting the type that I saw on television.

Will & Grace was an incredibly successful sitcom with two leading gay characters. The show focused on the tight friendship of Will and Grace. Will was gay and Grace was straight. They lived in their amazing New York apartment and led wonderful and hilarious lives. Will was the only gay character I knew at the time who wasn't overly flamboyant or effeminate. He was a lawyer, spent most of his life around straight people, and for much of the show his sexuality was barely an issue. His best friend, Jack, however, was an embodiment of the ridiculous stereotype of a gay man. Jack was a fool, but also incredibly sexually active.

This was another aspect of gay culture that perplexed me: was monogamy in the minority in gay relationships? Would I be expected to have multiple partners? Would my eventual partner come into the relationship expecting to be able to have sex with other people?

Frustratingly, there was little information to answer my questions, and I was too scared to reach out to anyone. My parents had given absolutely no indication that they would have anything less than an indifferent reaction to me being gay. Despite this, I was certain that they would reject me and I would disappoint them both. I was convinced the world was against me.

In an early episode of *Will & Grace*, Jack is forced to come out to his mother after decades of hiding from her. The mother is shocked but ultimately loving. I just happened to show that emotional episode to my mother one evening. She displayed no reaction. In the silence between us, it must have been obvious to her what I was trying to deal with in my head, but I made it incredibly difficult for my parents to talk to me. I would only reply in frustrated grunts to even the simplest of requests. I was a permanently melancholic force around the household, and I growled at anyone who came close. My parents had little option but to give me space. If they hadn't, I might have fallen into the stereotype that countless teenagers do: sneaking out of home to find solace for confusion.

Perhaps a wine at the end of the day would've calmed me down a bit, but even this idea was terrifying to me. The possibility of becoming drunk and losing control over my uptight performance in front of anyone was too much of a risk. I had never had a drink and had no interest in changing that.

As the days marched on, I built up a picture of what it meant to be gay, informed by porn and a lot of television. I thought it meant I had to be promiscuous, visiting bath houses, parks and public toilets to engage in 'hot love'. I found this idea a little uncomfortable, but I was convinced I could come to terms with it, given the hormonal clusterfuck that was going on inside my body that meant I would happily hump a bag of flour if it meant bringing some relief to my drive. I would also have to be witty, sharp and sarcastic. This was fine with me: it was the performance I'd been giving for years. This persona would keep me a safe distance from any true intimacy with anyone, something I believed was essential to my personal safety.

But the most attractive part of the picture I was building was the idea that I could become a girl's best friend and have an emotionally intimate relationship with a woman without having sex with her. If I was gay, it meant women wouldn't expect anything other than friendship from me. My female relationships could become wonderfully uncomplicated if the idea of attraction was not an issue. Maybe I would finally find a best friend, a sister of sorts, that I could rely on and talk to without becoming tangled in romance. This thought came as a sharp relief. Generally speaking, I found it much easier to be friends with girls than with guys. And anything that made my friendships with women easier was a bonus.

But...I could imagine myself sleeping with a woman. So was I still straight?

I was rubbish at sport, and always had been.

I had an interest in theatre and was partial to the odd musical.

I wore cologne and dressed in colourful clothes.

Most damningly, while I was still attracted to them, I was terrified of any kind of romantic relationship with women.

I found men attractive and had fantasies about them.

With these facts in mind, it seemed I had no option other than to be gay.

This was terrifying. Wouldn't I have to go out to nightclubs and somehow learn the rules of body glitter? Wouldn't I have to develop a taste for disco music, and lose any kind of strength in my inner-wrist? Would I have to wear things with feathers, and speak with a lisp and shout things like 'Hey, gurl!'?

Months before the panic attack, I started making secret deals with myself. If I was still attracted to a guy in a month and I hadn't found a girl I liked, that was it: I was gay. Decision made. The month would come and go and I would extend the deadline, certain that more information was on the way. None came.

I would lie awake at night and build fantasies that were rich and giddy with lies. I would avoid the whole issue by running away from everyone I knew. I would start anew, free of any of my previous ties to who I was. I'd find a girl. I'd build a home. We'd have kids. I'd be fine. I would have a beautiful life...

Until the morning I couldn't move.

I ended up staying at home for a fortnight. The time spent in isolation made the hopelessness of the situation desperately apparent.

I wasn't ready to go to any kind of doctor, but I found therapy in television shows and old movie favourites like *Star Wars* and *Harry Potter*, and the comedy of Billy Connolly. For what it's worth, I've found solace in certain shows and comedians again and again in my darkest hours. I end up cemented to the couch, gazing at the television. Billy Connolly, Eddie Izzard, and John Clarke have all helped me get out of bed at one time or another. Comedians are effective antidepressants. That's their job.

So, with no other option, I went back to school two weeks after that first panic attack in the shower. I was a little more ready to accept the idea that I was gay. The time of rest had allowed me to gather enough strength to get through the final weeks of school, and I plunged back into the miasma with my mask safely resecured.

What other option did I have?

I put myself to work, throwing myself into everything I could. That final block of year twelve passed in a dizzying swirl of activity. Students around me regularly crumpled into tears. It was a sad and joyful and beautiful time of our lives. We were leaving this place that I had once dreaded. We were on the cusp of adulthood. We reflected. We prayed. We celebrated.

I felt nothing. I was still in shellshock from the time in bed. Nevertheless, Crazy Drama Dave lived on. But each day ended with a nagging question in my brain. Would anyone at school accept me if they knew I was gay?

In one of the final English classes for year twelve, I was sitting beside a girl called Monica. Monica and I had a heap of classes together, so we knew each other quite well. Monica was everything I'm not: she was full of confidence, she was sexually active, and she wasn't terribly afraid of what anybody thought of her. We weren't besties, but she was a mate.

We were talking about her long-term boyfriend, and the latest in a series of troubles they were having— each one seemingly more traumatising than the last, but easily forgotten in the face of young love. I was playing my role perfectly, being a very supportive friend and giving out my opinion relentlessly. Inside, I was awed at the length and passion of the relationship, something I desperately longed for.

'The sex is amazing,' she said.

I made some non-specific sound of acknowledgment.

'When did you lose your virginity, Dave?' she asked, with perfect sincerity.

Oh, Jesus. How do you play this one, Dave? A few responses ran through my mind, none of which made much sense:

I could give a hearty chuckle and a wink: 'When *didn't* I lose my virginity?' (What? What does that even mean?)

I could try to seize the moment as an opportunity to flirt, do my best toothy grin and reply, 'Well, what are you doing in the next five minutes?'

I could upturn the table and scream in her face: 'Ya MUM'S virginity!' and run out of the room.

None of these options seemed particularly feasible, so I was left with the blunt truth.

'I...ah...haven't yet.'

'*What?!*' she suddenly screamed at maximum volume. 'Dave! You're missing out!'

I squirmed, and told her to shoosh. Kids around us were raising their eyebrows.

I had a choice here, a perfect opportunity to come out. I did the calculations in my head. Monica was undeniably liberal and sexually open. She was not a terribly close friend, and if I lost her to this revelation, it would be a major blow, but not heart-wrenching devastation. The only real risk was that she might tell other people.

Before I could think too much, I grabbed a pen and wrote a small note on the side of her page.

'Actually,' it said, in tiny blue scrawl, 'I think I might be gay.'

She read it and looked up at me, her face arching in surprise and instant recognition. I took the pen and furiously crossed out my confession. It was one of the few times I had been honest about my feelings in years. It was terrifying.

'That makes sense,' she said. And then, amazingly, 'You okay?'

I smiled, and nodded. 'Yeah.'

'I won't tell anyone.'

'Thanks.'

'Do you like anyone?'

I laughed. 'No, not really.'

'When you go to uni, you'll have *heaps* of options.'

I shrugged. 'Maybe.'

And then we went back to talking about her boyfriend.

Monica was the best. She was reassuring. She didn't tell anyone, and her behaviour towards me didn't change. She was extraordinarily positive. She didn't joke about it until I was ready to joke about it. It was a huge relief.

I realised that I had grossly underestimated the kindness of the people around me, and their interest in my wellbeing. The world was a nicer place than I had made it out to be.

Over the final few months of high school, I gradually came out to a wider group of my friends. Each coming out was easier than the last. I was overwhelmed with feelings of sheer disbelief. No one had run away! No one cared one way or the other!

But I was yet to tell the people whose responses I feared the most: Mum and Dad, and Simon.

In those final months of year twelve, I gave a pitch-perfect performance as Crazy Drama Dave at school. At home, I was a silent brooding shadow. I was full of raw self-hatred. I was terrified of the oblivion that was to follow graduation; I was certain I would plummet into nothingness. I was miserable. I had finally been open with some of my friends, and now it was only a matter of weeks before we were all separated.

There was that other small thing, of course: I had to decide what I wanted to do with the rest of my life.

A couple of years earlier, after Mary and Mrs Coates left, the school debating team had fallen by the wayside. Simon became obsessed with grades and started to bow out of any extra-curricula activities, seeing them as distractions.

Legal Studies was one of my senior subjects, and I had taken up mooting. Mooting is basically arguing fake law cases that are designed to groom up-and-coming lawyers. It's like debating, but with more complex rules. It required weeks of preparation for a single case, including reading other law cases for examples of precedence. I loved the research aspect of it and the improvisational nature of the final delivery. The judge could interrupt your case at any time and ask any number of questions, demanding that you knew your case history in fine detail and could argue out any number of legal technicalities.

I was Junior Counsel in year eleven and Senior Counsel in year twelve, and was awarded the best in the state in both roles. The whole exercise was run by a very posh university, and the awards garnered me some attention. One day my mooting coach pulled me aside.

'You know, Dave,' he began, 'with awards like these you'd be neatly placed for a scholarship. You'd be a great lawyer.'

'Oh,' I said, surprised. 'Thanks. I hadn't really thought about it.'

'You should. You'd be insane to turn down an

opportunity like that. It's the best university for law, and it'd be the start of a *very* lucrative career.'

I hadn't thought about my future in concrete detail. I had plans, but they were vague. This was despite my teachers and peers asking me constantly, 'What are you going to do when you graduate?'

Way back at the start of high school, I had asked Simon what he wanted to be when he grew up. It was a playful and light-hearted question, but Simon proceeded to lay out his ten-year plan for becoming a member of the defence force. At the age of thirteen, Simon already knew which subjects he would choose, and what marks he needed to get in each of his exams. Five years on, Simon's life was on schedule. I didn't know what the hell was going on with mine.

Law seemed like a reasonable option. It involved a combination of human relationships, communications and problem-solving. Legal Studies was fun: most of my mates were in the class with me. And I was good at it. There was also a good chance that I'd get a scholarship and there would be no financial cost. Plus, Will from *Will & Grace* was a lawyer, so I knew gay people could be lawyers. It was obvious.

Ironically, given all of my uncomfortable experiences with psychologists, I also had a minor interest in psychology. The thing that fascinated me was the way human minds work. Helping people with depression, like my mother and Tiff and Mary (and myself), seemed to be a noble undertaking, and one I thought I would be good at. My endless drive to help people might actually be put to good use.

And then there was drama.

I was shocked to find you could actually study it at university. You could do 'theatre studies'. I had no idea what 'theatre studies' meant, but it sounded exciting. It was a path that could lead to drama teaching, and I realised, somewhat quietly, that I could probably do that and enjoy myself. Becoming someone like Mr or Mrs Coates meant writing shows and producing them every year, and spending hours of time in drama class-rooms, which were my favourite places on earth.

I researched what doing 'theatre studies' might actually mean and I came across the degree in acting and performance.

A whole degree in *acting*? Three years of just *performing*? And then to be an actor, in film, or TV or the theatre, as a *job*?

The time came to fill out the university application forms. With the paperwork laid out, Mum and Dad sat down with me to go through the university guide.

'What are you thinking?' Dad asked.

'Theatre. Psychology. Law,' I replied. This was no surprise to my parents. They nodded.

And then they did something that I've since realised is a complete rarity.

They smiled warmly and said, 'Do whatever makes you happy.'

So I took their advice. I had to put in six options. I put psychology in the last two spots, law in the middle two, and acting and theatre at the top.

Each senior student was required to see a school counsellor to go over their preferences before they submitted them. I took my filled-out sheet into the counsellor's office to talk to a mild-mannered middle-aged woman whom I'd never met before.

'Okay, David. Let's have a look.'

I gave her the sheet.

'Okay, now I see you've put down theatre for the first two options, but that's going to be terribly difficult to find a job in, isn't it? So I think law will be best. Your grades are excellent. Here we go.'

She produced a red pen and, right in front of me, crossed out the theatre options on the page.

I nodded warmly. 'Thanks so much,' I said. 'You're very right.'

I walked out of the room and threw the paper in the bin.

Stupid bitch.

There was no way I was doing anything *but* theatre now.

10

How to Survive Year Twelve

Graduating from my high school involved more cere-
monies and rituals than applying for a licence to kill. In
the space of about a fortnight we had a senior retreat,
a valedictorian dinner, a commencement address, the
leadership handover, an awards night, a graduation
mass, a senior leadership mass, the sacrificing of a small
goat and a dance offering to the Gods of Olympus.

Before we were finally set free to wreak havoc on
the world, we were taken away for one last school camp.
This was the senior retreat: an emotional three-day trip,
carefully curated by the staff as a time for reflection.
It was the type of thing where the word 'journey' was

used every two minutes.

We split into close 'sharing' groups. At first these sessions fell victim to general teenage indifference. We were used to being pushed around and told to reflect and pray, and we weren't that bothered by it. But a few things happened that changed our minds.

The first was a couple of teachers telling us their life stories. They got up in front of us all and told of teenage struggles that seemed markedly difficult and way tougher than my own troubles. I was astonished. Poverty, family deaths, miscarriages and abuse were all talked about. I had never thought that the people around me were also human beings with their own demons to deal with. But, speaking about it now, in their middle age, they showed remarkable resilience. I couldn't work it out—how could they stand there and smile? How could they get over it? They each ended up so normal, with a spouse and kids and a regular job.

I remained unconvinced that my life could have the same fate. I felt I was destined to be unhappy and abnormal, in one way or another, for the rest of my life.

I didn't share this with the group. My armour was too tight.

Other students began to open up, however, and one of them was Ray.

Ray, darling cheese-loving Ray, who I had abandoned now for more than four years. While I had climbed the social ladder, Ray had remained on that bottom rung. His slow speech and frequent interruptions in class meant that he was the victim of much eye-rolling frustration. His lack of hygiene meant people were visibly reluctant to sit next to him. The original novelty of his inability to discuss anything other than cheese, *Pokémon* and *Austin Powers* disappeared quickly, and Ray was left in isolation.

In his group at retreat, Ray confessed he had no idea what his life would be like after school. He admitted to having attempted suicide.

The worst thing was that I wasn't surprised. I felt guilty for all of the times that I had turned my back on him, starting in those early days in our very first year when Simon had been so rude. But my regret came too late. We were only weeks away from the end of school, and nothing could undo the last five years of Ray's silent unhappiness.

On the final night of the retreat, each student was given a gift: a collection of letters, written by parents and relatives in secret. Inside my parcel I received heartfelt notes from my extended family and my parents. They were funny and moving, and there were lines that brought me to quiet tears.

'There are a lot of ideas out there of what a man should be,' Dad wrote, 'and most of them are bullshit.

What counts is character. And, by God, you've got a lot of that.'

'You are an excellent brother,' Mum wrote, 'and the boys are incredibly lucky to have you in their lives.'

I was shocked. I had spent so many hours contemplating how my parents didn't love me, or how they were incapable of understanding the *real* me. I hadn't spent nearly enough time considering how they actually felt. That I was capable of being loved was a genuine surprise.

The stream of exercises on those retreat days caused me to look back on the past five years. The miserable tale of hardship and trauma that I had been telling myself for years (awful boyfriend, bully victim and loser) began to morph when I changed perspective. I wasn't nearly as alone in the world as I had thought I was. Although I had constantly insisted I never needed help and that I was 'fine', I had been very lucky always to have had assistance available to me.

A small handful of teachers remained personally invested in me right through high school. Some offered words of advice about Mary and regularly asked about my life at home. Mr and Mrs Coates both went out of their way to give me the opportunities they felt I deserved. There were many other teachers who would've gone above and beyond to try to give me the tools I needed to gain a brighter outlook. And, ultimately, as their letters proved, Mum and Dad were willing and enthusiastic to help at any turn.

I had spent the years of my high-school life feeling isolated, assuming that I was alone in my struggles. I had told myself, repeatedly, that I had nowhere to go and no one to reach out to. This is the biggest mistake of the anxious or depressive mind. I had assumed I was alone. I'd fallen into this trap like a true disciple of negativity.

I realised all of this just as the structure and support of school was about to become unavailable to me.

∿∿∿

'Okay,' he says. 'What have you got for us?'

The man in front of me is built like a tank. He takes theatre *very* seriously. He's the head of acting at the university where I'm auditioning. His tone is flat. The message is clear. I'm here to prove something to him.

My contemporary monologue is Doug, from a play called *Cosi* by Louis Nowra. Doug is a pyromaniac who has set fire to a cat. Easy. I just play crazy. I start whizzing through the monologue with barely a breath, trying to control my nerves.

He stops me before I'm forty seconds in.

'Right,' he says, approaching. 'I want you to do that again.' He's just picked up a large stick. 'But I need you to be more threatening.' He's swinging the stick around threateningly. 'I want you to scare us.' He's looking at me with that stick. 'It's a threatening character.' The stick is very large. 'Okay?' he hands me the stick.

I nod. Smile.

Threatening. What could be easier?

I begin.

This time, it's only twenty seconds. He stops me.

'No,' he shakes his head. 'It's about showing us you're in control.' He approaches again, gets close to my face. 'Don't back down. Put all your energy forwards.'

'Ah,' I say, like I suddenly know what he is talking about. 'Yep. No worries.'

Right. Okay. Forwards. I'm trying to ignore the fear-induced urine that's threatening to put its energy forwards in my pants.

I begin. This time, I get through the whole thing, but I can feel that I'm not delivering what he wants. His sharp nod and grimace confirms it.

'Good. Your Shakespeare?'

It's from *Henry VII*. I haven't read the whole play and I only kind of vaguely know what I'm saying. But I deliver it.

'Great. Thanks very much.'

I'm done. Less than ten minutes. I already know that I'm not in the acting course. I'm not sure why. The experience of auditioning is like nothing I've encountered at school, where I easily picked up the lead in the school musical. That may have had a lot to do with the fact that there were no other males in my year level doing drama, but, still, I was shocked by the experience I'd just had.

Bizarrely enough, acting requires a very real and tangible connection to one's true self.

Fat chance.

I barely had time to reflect on my failure. Less than half an hour later and just a few metres down the hall, I had a far more friendly interview for the theatre studies course. The acting audition had taken place in the theatre: a large, intimidating space where the seats were raked in such a way to look down upon the performers and shrink their confidence. My interview for theatre studies was in a small studio. A beaming and relaxed woman called Donna welcomed me. We sat down opposite each other.

'Fuck,' she muttered, under her breath, flicking through some papers. 'I'm so sorry, Dave. I've left your papers on my desk. I'll be back in a tick.'

She rushed out of the room. I was alarmed by this quick interaction for many reasons.

1. A teacher had sworn at me. And not half-heartedly. It was a proper, meaningful 'fuck'. I'd been at school for twelve years, the last five of them in the Catholic education system, and I had never heard a teacher swear. Except for my music teacher in year eight,

who once chastised a group of boys for 'pissing around'. The slip had caused a major scandal that lasted for the rest of the term.

2. She had called me Dave, as if we were old friends. I had come in expecting to be judged for my academic and theatrical merit, but she seemed far too relaxed for this to be the case.

3. My 'papers' included a short essay that all prospective theatre-studies students were required to write. Trouble was, I had handed mine in late. I'd had so much warning from high-school teachers that a university-level institution wouldn't put up with tardiness or laziness of any kind that I was positive that my late submission would make me ineligible for the course. I had written a simple and heartfelt note of apology to accompany the essay, promising that such lateness was deeply unusual and not at all indicative of my work ethic. I knew she was about to see that note. She would return to the room and probably ask me to leave.

4. She swore. Fuck. She said fuck.

My alarm didn't last long. Donna rushed back into the studio. She had a kind face and a sharp shock of brown hair. She was dressed elegantly but simply in a loose grey jumper and dark jeans. Her face was beautifully expressive, making her intensely charismatic. She asked me several questions and listened intently to my answers. We even managed to make each other laugh a few times. And when we did, I was rewarded with a free and infectious guffaw from her. She looked at the note of apology I had attached to my essay, smiled and said, 'That's sweet.' Then she put the note aside and didn't refer to it again.

The monologue I had prepared for Donna was quite different from the pyromaniac performance. Wanting to show extra creative zeal that was more appropriate for the course, I had created a monologue from the various speeches of Prior Walter, the lead character in my favourite play at the time, *Angels in America* by Tony Kusher. (It's filled to the brim with characters struggling with their sexuality.)

Donna smiled as I performed it, and we talked about it in depth afterwards. The entire exchange would've only been fifteen minutes, but I left the conversation feeling good. The acting course was completely forgotten. The only thing I wanted to do was theatre studies.

A week later, as school was wrapping up, I was pleased to receive my offer in the mail. Just like that my future was decided. Theatre studies. I accepted the offer.

Two months later, offers for psychology and law came in the mail. I didn't think twice. I knew I had made the right decision.

The theatre studies course also included the option of following it with a year studying education, to become a teacher. So, should I indeed graduate and discover myself instantly poor and homeless as my career counsellor had predicted, I could go back to study and become a drama teacher. I had very little idea of what I really wanted to do with my life, but drama was the only thing that really made my heart bounce.

My principal, teachers and some members of my family baulked at my commitment to almost certain poverty, especially in light of the legal pathway and its promise of financial success that was open to me. But my parents insisted that I choose the pathway that provided me with the most happiness (and to keep the teaching option open for as long as possible). If it wasn't for my parents, I would've almost certainly surrendered to the pressure and a career plan that was far more 'sensible', but filled with far less joy.

I'd now like to tell you one of the worst-kept secrets in education. The endless exams, numbers and streams of bureaucracy that year-twelve kids are made to suffer actually mean very little in the real world. They may help you get into a university in the months immediately following your secondary graduation, but that's about all they're good for. The gap between an 'A' grade and a 'B' doesn't ruin your life.

I was bewildered by some of my classmates'

behaviour. Having been told that the last two months of high school would dictate their success as human beings *for the rest of their lives*, many collapsed in stress and despair. Some threw their hands up without even trying, finding it easier to fail without effort than to risk academic rejection.

In the years since graduating with my theatre degree, I have spent long months in poverty. These periods were filled with stress, but also abundant joy at being involved in an industry that I loved. Since that time, I have built a stable and robust career.

I wish I could say that my depressive days were over by the time I finished year twelve, but the worst was yet to come. If I had faced the same challenges that I was to encounter in my post-high-school years while working in a job that I found financially but not spiritually rewarding, I would likely no longer be living.

I'm not exaggerating. I would have died.

At seventeen, I had all kinds of delusions about the type of person that I was. But I was smart enough, thanks to my parents, to understand one golden truth: I was not my grades. I was not my career. To put my identity down to a number on a piece of paper was an insult to the wild spaciousness of education, but also to the largeness of my true self. Working hard is a great and necessary thing, but there are elements that are always going to be out of our control, and failure is incredibly important and also temporary.

I was blessed to have been taught these lessons from my parents at an early age. I only wish I had listened to them deeper in my heart and applied them to other aspects of my life. As I stood on the cusp of high school graduation, however, there was a lot I had yet to figure out.

For example, I was still to find a shag.

Out

In the months immediately following graduation, a lot happened to my classmates.

A young bully became a young father.

A shot-put superstar was forced to deal with the sudden death of his mother.

A couple of high-school sweethearts got engaged.

And most of the year level got well and truly sloshed at schoolies.

I stayed at home and waited the four months before university began. I spent most of the time in my bedroom, doing pretty much what I did during my hiatus from existence a few weeks earlier. A lot of TV, a lot of dark thoughts, and very little interaction with the outside world.

Mum pushed me once again to go to a psychologist. I wasn't eating and I was barely moving. With nothing but time to kill, and feeling completely miserable, I relented.

This was how I met Gary. Gary was cool. He didn't patronise me. He didn't have ye olde maps on the walls. He was in a band and he had Tolkien on his bookshelf. I felt like he listened to me. He was my first really positive experience with a psychologist, and I grew to trust him. I began to talk about my most urgent concern.

I'd had unexpected support from a few classmates when I came out in the last few weeks of school, but I had saved the most dreaded announcements for last.

Mum, Dad and Simon needed to be told. I felt that if I was able to be honest with them I might experience some kind of liberation, even though I desperately feared each of their reactions.

I knew I would lose at least one of them.

∧∧∧

I came out to Mum in the middle of the night.

We were up having a long conversation about some of her troubles. Mum was perpetually unhappy, and it was something that I was simultaneously frustrated by and sympathetic to. The world had been hard on Mum in all sorts of ways, and I did my best to help her. This particular evening she had been crying, and we talked for hours.

Exhausted by her tears, she got up to go to bed. It was about two o'clock, and she would be up in a few hours. Mum liked to garden at dawn before launching into a retinue of household chores.

As we wandered to the kitchen, Mum asked how I was. I shrugged, non-committed, and turned around to face her. She was in the lounge room, in darkness, peering at me in the dim kitchen. I made a decision.

'Mum,' I said. 'I think I'm probably gay.'

She nodded, and with barely a pause said, 'Well that's fine.' Her voice pitched upwards, as if she was trying to convince herself, and desperate to convince me.

'That's fine,' she said again, more certain. And she smiled. 'I'm not surprised.'

And then we said goodnight and went to bed.

I knew it was only a matter of hours until my father heard the news.

〰〰〰

A few days later, Dad and I were in the car.

'Are you ready for an awkward conversation?' he

asked with an embarrassed laugh.

Holy fuck, he's bringing it up. It's happening now. Shit, it's happening now.

'Um. Yeah?'

He was so uncomfortable. I'd never seen my dad more uncomfortable.

'Mum tells me, I hope you don't mind—'

Why would I mind? Jesus, Mum, why would I object to that in anyway?

'Mum tells me you might be gay. And I just wanted to let you know that that's fine with me, that's fine.'

Silence. This is good. I think this is good. Is this good?

'Okay,' I say.

'But I also wanted to let you know that you're young. You've got time. And you might want to experiment a little more before you say—'

'I'm pretty certain,' I interrupt.

So he's not fine. He's in denial. Mum probably is too. Right. They think it's a phase.

Even though I had never had a kiss, let alone a sexual experience with either a man or a woman, I was unwilling to tolerate even the faintest notion that I might simply be confused. I was so sick of confusion. I needed certainty. The internet research and countless videos and television I watched taught me that parents often responded to their child's coming out with the denial-laden 'it's just a phase'. According to my research, this was pure intolerance and needed to be combated.

It was not a phase. It was me.

I was defensive, but I was also surprised that I hadn't been kicked out of home or shunned.

Let's face it, my parents had always been nothing but supportive, and while Dad was a little hesitant, he certainly wasn't offended. Mum was more worried about other friends' or neighbours' reactions, but by this point I'd had enough positive coming-out experiences to not waste time worrying about neighbourhood gossip.

But the real test was always going to be Simon.

I told him a few weeks after schoolies.

Over the internet.

Good choices, Dave.

His schoolies experience had been a blur of drinking, cheap food and sunburn. Now he was getting ready to leave for Canberra to study engineering in the defence force.

'It was pretty wild,' he types.

'Did you hook up with anyone?'

'I met a girl called Melissa.'

'Cool.'

'We mucked around a bit.'

'Still talking?'

'Yeah, she's online now actually. We're talking.'

'Ooooooo!!!!!!'

I tried not to be jealous of Simon's easy ability to end up 'mucking around' with someone. The idea of going to schoolies and striking up a conversation with a drunk stranger made my stomach turn. But Simon was happy. Good for him.

A few minutes pass. He must be busy chatting with Melissa.

I type, 'What's Melissa like?' Just as a question pops up from him.

'What's been happening with you?'

Now's the time to tell him. Before I think, I type, 'I'm pretty sure I'm gay.'

The words blink onto the screen, set into pixelated stone, never to be erased. There's no going back.

Long seconds tick past. My confession hangs there, begging for a reply.

Then: 'She's from the Sunshine Coast. She's going to do engineering or something down in New South Wales. We might be able to see each other, but I don't know how it'll work.'

Shit. Did he not see it? Or has he seen it and chosen to ignore it?

'Cool,' I type back nervously. I don't know how to proceed. Do we just keep talking about Melissa like I *haven't* just said I'm gay? Was this it? Was it over? Do I type it again?

A message appears on the screen.

'Are you excited to meet the other fags at drama school?' He punctuates the thought with a 😮.

I read it three times. The first time I'm confused. The second time I'm hurt. The third time I'm angry.

'That's shitty,' I say.

There's nothing for a long time. He's probably laughing with Melissa now, telling her his best friend's a faggot.

'Jeez,' he types, 'I was just joking.'

'It's not funny.'

'Stop being a girl.'

That's it. I'm sick of being told I'm a woman, or a fag. And I'm sick of Simon's bullshit. I close the laptop and sit back in my chair.

I go over the conversation in my mind. I don't know whether the face meant Simon's disgust or if it was supposed to be my face offering a blow job.

I need support. I knew he'd be a douche about it. I feel my throat tighten, and my eyes begin to sting.

We'd seen each other almost every day for five years.

I convinced myself I was better off without him anyway.

Simon was the last point of contact I had with high school. None of my previous classmates would be studying in the local arts faculty, let alone in my course. I would be alone. It was a chance to start again.

Crazy Drama Dave could finally retire.

A part of me was relieved. The performance had been exhausting. And now I was 'out', I felt way more at ease with the possibility of making new female friends.

But would I even be able to make new friends? I would be completely alone at university. And without Crazy Drama Dave, would I just return to being the scared thirteen year old who was picked on and hid out in the library? Would I plummet to the bottom of the social ladder again?

I desperately needed a new personality.

I decided to make my new-found sexuality the cornerstone of the new me. Confident, proud, energetic and gay. Crazy Drama Dave was dead. Gay Dave had risen.

I was lucky. I landed in the Willy Wonka Chocolate Factory of sexual confusion: a university theatre department.

12

All the Feels

In drama school you learn how to feel things. A lot. All the time. My first fortnight at uni was like emotional boot camp—the exact kick in the heart that I needed to restart the sense of who I was.

We spent most of the first semester in a small room of painted-brown concrete, developing a show for young children. The quickest way to get to know someone is to create something with them, so our merry band of seventeen strangers quickly became a chaotic orgy of liberated outcasts. We were all outsiders, we were all geeks, and we had all found safety and refuge in the drama room at school. Now we were in a drama class that never ended. In fact, we were going to build our lives into a drama class that never ended.

Heaven, right?

There were a lot of feelings.

A lot.

And we were instructed to shout these feelings at top volume. Into a wall. Or to a partner on the other side of the room. Now with a partner, joining hands, chanting together to specific rhythms. Now as an animal. A shadow. Just syllables. Vowels. Consonants. Just as feelings. Noises. A tree. A tree in the wind. The feeling of wind.

Feelings! So many feels!

In between rehearsals we talked. We were seventeen drama nerds, all from different places, but we talked about high school as if we had managed to survive a war. There was the softly spoken young man who said he turned to White Pride and Hitler speeches in year ten in an attempt to make the bullies scared of him. The girl who self-harmed by heating forks over a candle flame and then branding herself, letting the burn marks sink into her skin. There was the charismatic boy who told us he had made it through the last few years of high school by drinking a bottle of cheap red wine every day.

That last one was Ravi.

I spent most of my uni years wanting to be Ravi. He was charming, handsome and exotic, and loved.

Ravi laughed. A lot. His humour was infectious. And he was sexually free and liberated, or at least he appeared to be. With a bit of pushing, he would hint at sexual encounters with beautiful strangers. We would all sit around him, enthralled. I wanted to be Ravi.

I owned gay like a badge, marching forth and letting it lead my personality. Ravi had enough confidence to shrug in the face of his bisexuality and happily carry on. I hadn't figured out how to do that yet, and it drove me nuts. I only knew how to be an outspoken gay guy, but Ravi was a relaxed gay (or bi, depending on his mood) guy. Of course, he was coming from an equally confusing time at high school, but he seemed far more relaxed about the entire thing.

Friendship groups quickly formed, and I attached myself to Ravi like we were long-lost brothers. Ravi—strong, chaotic, sensitive, almost certainly a Time Lord. Ravi would come to uni cloaked in a pashmina he'd picked up from the op shop. He would take us on journeys through the town at night, finding little niches of parks with the best playgrounds, which I had never seen. He'd show us how to get to the town's water tower and to hop, skip and jump our way to the top. Ravi and I had grown up in the same town, but in very different places. My bedroom had been my escape. For Ravi, the whole town was his hidey-hole.

I also became friends with Nina. Short-haired,

sharp-witted, a simmering fighter. She's a Legolas: a nimble elf, a precise marksman, an agile foe. Nina is one of the smartest people I've ever met. Her cutting, dry humour was fantastic in a drama class: she could dismantle even the faintest whiff of bullshit with the shortest utterance. She'd face up to the lecturers ready for any challenge, and she was rewarded. Beneath her thick armour beat a heart of fierce loyalty; she had a softness and deep affection for the special few she loved. She was the first one in the class that I came out to.

Mainly because she asked.

'You're gay, right?'

That's how Nina asks.

'Yeah,' I said.

And that was it. I was out at uni. I was officially Gay Dave. I was Gay Dave with a merry bunch of friends.

The final friend to join this furious foursome was Amber. Amber was older than us by a couple of years. She had dabbled in various certificate courses before finally landing in the theatre course. Quiet, funny and smart, Amber was a perfect Hermione Granger. Her stability and calm influenced us all. She was frightened of the world, but she was worshipped by our class as it quickly became obvious that Amber knew how to organise a production schedule better than anyone else. In fact, Amber knew how to organise most things better than anyone. Ever. When she smiled or giggled, she hid her face, as though she was scared that you might see her feelings underneath. She wore black. A lot.

So, Gay Dave joined Hermione (Amber), Legolas (Nina) and The Doctor (Ravi). The experience of creating the children's show bound us together quickly. When we finished, we set about putting on an after-party that would become legendary in the halls of the arts faculty. Absolutely everyone was invited.

There were other, older gay guys at uni. Maybe this party would be the point where I would get some sex.

I humbly asked my parents to buy me a sixpack of Vodka Cruisers. I didn't have a driver's licence and wasn't yet eighteen. I had no idea what Vodka Cruisers were. I had never drunk alcohol before. But Nina and Amber advised me to invest. Everyone would be drunk at the party.

I had kept myself locked away for years, certain that I didn't like company. It all seemed too intimidating. But I really liked these people, and there seemed to be a chance for the sexy times that I had dreamed of for years.

What was the paradise that lay ahead?

᙭᙭᙭

Turns out paradise smells faintly of vomit and is very loud. It's also a weird kind of clumsy soft porn that no one would ever be interested in watching. This was a university party. This is what I had been missing out on.

We were in someone's driveway. Generic, pulsing music thudded out of the interior of the house. We drank. And talked. And somewhere, somehow, someone suggested spin the bottle. And I found myself sitting in a circle, watching an empty Vodka Cruiser spin.

I had consumed one bottle, and I didn't feel particularly compelled to have another. I honestly couldn't tell whether I was actually drunk, or whether I was just playing drunk for the sake of the party, trying to convince myself as much as anyone else. Amber took to a bottle of rum and coke with vigour. Nina, the classiest of us all, had a bottle of white wine. Ravi had several bottles of watermelon schnapps, which he kept offering to everybody.

'Schnapps?!' he'd ask, excited. 'It's *well* tasty.'

I would be lying if I didn't say I was curious about kissing Ravi. He was a guy and he was bi. In fact, at this stage, we were the only open gays in our year. There were another couple of guys that everybody gossiped about, but no hard (get it?) evidence of homosexuality. There were gay guys in other years, from different parts of uni, but I hardly knew them. I wasn't about to go and try pashing older guys; I barely had my gay training wheels attached.

I didn't know where to begin. The whole thing

was confusing. I seemed to have missed the class where people were taught to flirt. I didn't understand it. Why would you flirt? Why not just ask the person if you could kiss them?

'Schnapps?!' Ravi offered to the people on either side of him in the circle. They each took a swig.

The vodka cruiser bottle was spun. The game was in motion.

I wasn't about to tell anyone I was a kiss virgin. I was struggling to remain cool without a drink in my hand, let alone with admitting that I'd never locked lips with anyone.

All seventeen of us, a ragged bunch of outcasts, gathered around the bottle. The anticipation was like Russian Roulette.

First up was Hannah, a manic-depressive mature-age student who had dyed her hair blue in an attempt to fit in with the younger group.

The bottle spun to the chants of oooos and ahhhhs. It began to slow down, threatening to stop right at me.

Was this it? Hannah? My first kiss? Really?

It stopped short, landing on the girl beside me. Carmen, a black-haired tattooed girl with a collection of piercings she'd done herself.

Hannah crawled over to Carmen and they stared at each other for a moment before drawing in for a kiss. We all erupted in cheers. The pair didn't let our applause go to waste. They stretched out their moment together, flicking their tongues into each other as we all laughed. It happened inches away from my face.

Hannah went back to her spot. 'You're an awesome kisser!' she said to Carmen.

'Schnapps?!' Ravi said, offering them the bottle.

We went round the circle. People were pashing without a second thought. Dan, formerly of White Pride, kissed Anna, the girl from New Zealand who smelt like onions. Sarah, the self-branding self-mutilator, kissed Russell, the musical theatre-loving bombastic boy who was very keen to tell us that he *wasn't gay at all*.

And so it went, missing me each time. I was simultaneously relieved and disappointed. Either way, it would be my turn soon, and I would spin the bottle, and it would, hopefully, for the love of God, land on Ravi. I wasn't sure if I was attracted to him, or whether I just didn't want to kiss anyone else.

It was my turn.

Ravi. Please.

The bottle felt cold in my hand. I took a deep breath, and spun.

Please, God, please. Just let it land on someone nice. And please don't let me be crap. Please don't let them laugh in my face. And what are *they* thinking? Is each person in the circle praying that it doesn't land on them? Are they all dreading the thought of my face pressed against theirs?

It passed Ravi once. Twice. Three times.

It began to slow.

This was my first kiss. A game of chance in a driveway, with one bottle of orange Vodka Cruiser in my belly.

I knew who it was going to be a second before it stopped. The bottle pointed accusingly at Anna. Onion girl.

I smiled at her. She smiled back. If she was disappointed, she didn't show it. My eyes flicked to Ravi, who smiled back sympathetically.

'Schnapps?!' he offered.

I almost took a swig, but I didn't, fearing that it would be rude to Anna, who was now crawling towards me with her bulky frame.

One moment she was an inch or two away, the next, her face was on mine. I realised that my lips were dry, and hers were ridiculously wet. I heard the crowd around us cheering. She opened her mouth and I felt her tongue on my lips, which I kept tighter than a cat's arse, not daring to let her enter. Finally it was over, and she drew away.

'You taste really nice,' she said.

'Thanks, so do you,' I said, not really thinking about it.

'You taste like orange.'

I shrugged and smiled, 'The vodka, probably.'

And then the game kept going.

That night I went from having kissed no one to kissing my entire class. Sixteen people in total. Ravi was my second kiss. His spin landed on me. My curious desire was about to be satisfied, and I wondered briefly whether this would be an evening we would both remember and laugh about in years to come. Was this how a romance would start?

Our lips drew together. His face was warm, and I realised instantly how different kissing a man was, if for no other reason than the mashing together of facial hair. I was confident now, and I felt 'experienced' having kissed a total of one other person. I opened my mouth and stabbed my tongue like a weapon into his face, but his lips remained tightly shut. I knew what that meant. It was exactly what I had done to Anna.

We drew apart and he smiled at me, and the game kept going.

I think I was disappointed. Possibly heartbroken. But the whole thing was so casual, so mundane, that I didn't know what to feel. And, as I kissed a dozen or more others, I began to ask myself why'd I'd been so worried all this time. Why had I longed for a romantic partner as though it was significant? Affection, for us, at that time, didn't seem to be too significant at all. In fact, it seemed like nothing. I suppose I should've felt relieved. But, somehow, I left feeling even more empty.

The cops turned up eventually. Ravi and a few others were talking about moving the party somewhere else, but I was done. It was midnight and I was cold. Any thin grasp the vodka had held on me was well and truly gone. Anna dropped me home. She'd been sober the entire time.

I crawled into bed and drifted into an uneasy sleep, the chanting and music still in my head. I was becoming a person I barely recognised.

For that, I was extremely grateful.

13

Fluids

'Right!' says Donna, clapping her hands with enthusiasm. 'Today we're going to talk about gender!'

She's standing at the front of the classroom, beaming at us. We're nearing the end of our first year, but we're still as green as ever, and I spot a few students around me shifting in their seats. Donna's lectures have a reputation for being mind-blowing for most, but confronting for a few.

For example, only a fortnight earlier we'd learnt about Beckett, a famous absurdist playwright. But with Beckett came a profound and quick education in existentialist philosophy and the work of some real party-throwers like Nietzsche, Satre, Kafka and Joyce. This upbeat crowd had gotten into a bit of hot water in their day. Nietzsche, for example, was extremely fond of telling people that God was dead. The idea was received with about as much enthusiasm as could be expected of a nineteenth-century crowd. There was a similar response among the young student body of this particular regional university arts department. Regardless, it was an important part of arts history, and Donna taught it with zeal.

Donna's classes were intense. She brought her flamboyant personality into the room and into her teaching. We would often leave the lecture theatre with cheeks sore from laughing. I found each lecture an amazing revelation. I was being introduced to new ideas almost every day.

But this class was slightly different. When Donna started talking about gender, we knew she was serious. Her PhD thesis, I had recently found out, was an examination of the role of boys in drama classrooms, which are usually filled with girls, and how young males relate to their gender. I realised that Donna might be able to help me with some of my confusion about being Gay Dave.

Or, on the other hand, I could just end up even more confused.

We were studying a play written in the spirit of 1970s feminism: *Cloud Nine* by Caryl Churchill. It's an amazing play for many reasons, but it raises some really tricky questions, like: what does being a man or woman even *mean*?!

Good question Caryl. Very good question.

In the final scenes of the play, a young man sits with his female friend. He's desperately confused. Uncertain of his preferences, desires, or standing in society, he concludes the scene with a bewildering realisation: 'I think I'm a lesbian.'

Wait.

Can men be lesbians?

Words like 'queer', 'bisexual', and 'gay' became a muddled mess in my head. Ravi, annoyingly, seemed to have it all figured out. I was fascinated and baffled.

Donna showed us a long series of slides that screwed with our heads. Jennifer Lopez with a beard. Still sexy. Still beautiful. But bearded. A still shot of pumped-up manly footballers, grabbing at each other and fondling, so close to kissing when you looked at it the right way.

I went home that day to a pile of *Men's Health* magazines, which I kept for the false promise that I would one day become a beautiful beefcake. But the six-pack abs and perfect pecs took on a new meaning now. They were a result of fashion. It was like a secret pact had been made by society, in some place far away, that said, 'This is what beautiful men look like, and this is how men behave.' And because of this, I had always felt like I wasn't beautiful, and I wasn't behaving as a real man should.

Never mind *Men's Health*, what about porn? Men with huge penises and tightly constructed bodies. Women with impossibly tidy vaginas and absurdly shaped breasts. What did it actually mean? And how did I fit in with any of it? What had porn been telling me about myself?

As I kept studying and talking with Ravi and Donna, I found the core of my thinking was changing. I had thought of gender as built on a rigid set of foundations: male, female; straight, gay. But my class's indiscriminate horniness and the perspective that came with gratuitous amount of study on the topic made me realise gender was far more fluid than that.

Who would I be, who would I be with, if I suddenly lost all of this baggage about stereotypes and was just me?

Within the year, I found myself in bed with two people at different times: one male, one female. I would very soon get answers to many of the questions that had bothered me since my first timid sexual experience in the bathroom when I was thirteen.

Whether I would like the answers was a whole other matter.

Meet James. Glasses, blond wispy hair, and always fashionable. And considerably more well-built than me. Despite his attention to style, James looked 'heterosexual' according to my unexperienced perception. He was in the theatre department, but he was in the stage-management section, which was made up of electricians, technicians and generally straight men.

James was also a perfectionist and was involved with every production the university did. The staff, constantly grateful for James's ceaseless volunteering, defined him as a 'special case', letting him stay extra late alone in the sound studio, armed with a can of Red Bull and an industry-standard sound desk. James would plug in his iPod and shake the walls of the studio with dubstep. In this private den, he would set about accomplishing whatever task was required of him. Amber would often join him.

Amber was also hard working, and as the two of us became closer, she asked me to help with a project that she and James were working on. So I found myself alone with James in the sound studio late one night. We were sharing a single computer screen and the long, dull task of waiting for huge amounts of data to be transferred from one hard drive to another.

It suddenly hit me: James and I would end up

making out. I was almost certain.

Don't ask me how. We weren't doing anything special. It was just in the way we smiled at each other and talked. *This* had been what I was missing for all these years. An alignment of deliberate attraction, one side not outweighing the other. I didn't feel guilty, pressured or ashamed. I knew, somehow, that James felt the same curiosity towards me.

So that's what it felt like, to find someone who feels the same way about you as you do about them.

It felt remarkable.

It felt grown up.

Meet Rachel: red hair, big smile, perfect teeth, wonderfully intelligent.

Rachel and I had known each other since high school. She had attended an all-girls' school across town, but we met at a school leaders' conference. We had fallen into an easy conversation, and the friendship grew from there. We'd see each other at events, and then spend a lot of time talking online. Rachel put a lot of pressure on herself to succeed academically. It was a notion derived from a high-powered career-focused mother and father, and I had been the most supportive friend that I knew how to be.

One evening, a few months after we'd first met, Rachel handed me a delicate handwritten note, politely informing me that she was in love with me.

I turned away her affection, clumsily and vaguely. But, because she was forgiving, because she listened to me, and perhaps because she was outside school and family, we stayed friends. She was supportive and kind, and she didn't blink when I came out. We continued our friendship when I went to uni, frequently sleeping at each other's house.

But I knew that the scales of the relationship were unbalanced. She was way more invested in me than I was in her.

Rachel gently insisted that I might not be gay.

James gently insisted that I was *very* gay.

With his hands.

James would keep touching me. Cheekily, briefly, in the most intimate of places, without any apology.

I went to Amber to talk about my feelings. I was attracted to James. It all seemed so funny and easy. But we barely saw each other outside uni—how would we make something happen?

I didn't realise that James was talking to Amber as well, asking her almost exactly the same question.

So, Amber did what Amber always did. She made plans. She invited us both around, with Ravi and Nina, for an 'Italian Night', a feast of food and booze.

'And if you get too drunk,' she said, 'don't worry,

there's the spare room.'

Amber knew exactly what she was doing.

Rachel also knew what she was doing.

For my birthday, she surprised me with an all-expenses-paid four-night trip to New Zealand for me, herself, and her mother.

I had never been outside Queensland.

We saw theatre, beautiful landscapes, and had a lot of fun. We stayed up late together in our hotel suite in Wellington, looking out over the lights of the city below. We sat on the couch, cups of tea in hand, and talked for hours, before the conversation disappeared and we simply sat in each other's company.

We shared a bed.

What did it matter? I was gay.

I shared a bed with James. Drunk on cheap booze and filled with enough carbohydrates to run a marathon, we squeezed into Amber's ridiculously small, single spare bed. Two grown men.

Then we pashed. A lot.

I hadn't asked about James's romantic history, nor had he enquired about mine, but we had somehow figured out that we were both very virginal. Our level of inexperience showed in our kissing.

I say kissing. It was more like eating. We both

thought bigger was better, and we almost unhinged our jaws in an attempt to swallow each other whole, like two snakes trying to stab the other to death.

I won't say it was romantic, but it stirred something in me. Afterwards, my mind was too busy to sleep, and I snuck out to the couch. I lay there, staring up at the ceiling, thinking of what had just happened, and why my jaw felt like it had been dislocated.

Weeks after the New Zealand trip, I was lying in Rachel's bed thinking about what could happen.

It was a hot night. Or warm. Either way, I complained that it was hot, and stripped down to my underwear.

'What would you say if I just walked in one day naked?' I asked.

Silence.

'I...I don't know.'

'It shouldn't matter, should it? I'm gay. We're friends.'

I could feel the heat of her body next to me. I could hear her thoughts, loud. I could see her outline in the dark.

'You don't know you're gay,' she said. 'And of course it matters. You'd be naked!'

I could do this, if I wanted to. Gender was fluid. Relationships were just ideas. This person was attracted to me. Somewhere inside of her, she wanted something from me. I could give her what she wanted.

'You're not experienced enough to know you're gay,' she continued.

I hadn't told her about James.

'I could become experienced. With you. I could try. And you could try too. We'd just be two friends. Helping each other.'

I was surprised at how aroused I was. I had a lot of control here. A lot of power.

Silence.

I spooned her, pressing the entirety of my near naked body into hers. We stayed like that for a long time.

No memory makes me more uncomfortable than this little scene. Me pushing the bounds of Rachel's affection. Using her as some kind of test to prove something about me. Could I be the sexually liberated guy I wanted to be?

I leant over, and moved my face towards hers.

'No,' she said.

She got up and left the room.

That wasn't how it was supposed to go.

This was how it was supposed to happen: James's twenty-first-birthday party, at his family's house, and he's conspired to have a spare bed for me in his room.

We're all there: Ravi, Amber, Nina and I, all drunk and laughing. But the whole night my head keeps going back to that spare bed and what James is expecting. The pressure feels air-tight, and I'm suddenly incredibly uninterested in sex.

Hours later, I return from brushing my teeth to see James already in his bed, looking at me, smiling.

'Come here,' he says.

He's bigger than me. Perhaps he'll try to force me if I don't say yes. We've play-wrestled before. But suddenly I feel sick at the thought.

I get into his bed and we spoon, but his hands tell me he's after more. I lie rigidly still, my heart beating furiously, ashamed of how soft I am when he feels me.

After too long, he gives up, and I crawl back to the mattress on the floor.

I give myself a good talking to: I'm gay, I should be loving this, I should be relentlessly horny and up for it all the time.

After all this time, all this anxiety, I can't just *not* be gay.

'I think I might be gay,' Rachel says to me.

We'd kept up a friendship, although we never shared a bed again after that night. But we spent a lot of time talking in the dark, looking out of windows, listening to music. And somewhere in there she told me about the night she swallowed all the pills she could find in the house, praying to go to sleep for a long time. Then she realised she couldn't feel her right foot, and she told her Mum, who rushed her to the hospital to get her stomach pumped.

That all happened somewhere in between New Zealand and the night I pressed myself up against her in the bed.

'Why didn't you tell me?' I asked.

She shrugged.

I thought we told each other everything.

Nina, Ravi, Amber and I told each other everything. Including how Ravi and James now had a fun playmate relationship, and they both enjoyed each other's bodies with great curiosity.

James and I fell out of sync.

Somehow, I'd managed to blow both my chances of some kind of physical relationship, including one with an incredibly sweet, smart gay man.

I should've been disappointed.

I was relieved.

14

Grown Up

I should mention, my parents were chillin' in the background this whole time. My brothers were there too, having spent most of the last five years in their bedroom, making their way through video games with religious fervour.

I had gone through my entire life without ever feeling the urge to move house and leave my family. I couldn't imagine a world without them. But now that I was at uni, I could see the freedom that Amber and others had was within reach. I could have a whole house to myself, or half a house, or a unit. Not just a room, but a whole *place.*

The idea that I *didn't* have my own place was outrageous, and I grew bitter about being trapped at home. I took my frustrations out on my family with my best angry-young-man act.

All the small things about my family that were once mere annoyances grew into thorny resentments. Perhaps this is part of growing up: you suddenly feel entitled to feeling let down, or hurt, by what your family wouldn't or couldn't supply to you.

It had happened one other time in my life, when I was just twelve. It was a Saturday afternoon. We'd travelled to the city with a singular purpose: to have our picture taken with the extended family. It was to be a gift for our grandmother.

The twins were just ten. I was also in primary school, not too far away from the moment when Cameron's hands would reach my neck and drag me across a certain visual arts table. The last time my family had been bundled into a photography studio, it had ended in disaster, with Andy and Chrissy spiralling into anxiety. I was already sceptical that my family could pretend to be normal for the sake of a photograph. Before the camera was even set up, there was trouble.

Chrissy wasn't happy. It had been a long, uncomfortable drive. He'd been made to wear an ironed shirt with buttons down the front and shoes that weren't comfortable. Chrissy's anxiety caused Andy's to rise in turn.

'Just shut up!' Andy told Chrissy repeatedly.

And so Chrissy squashed his anxiety further inside. He turned his attention to the hot red eczema marks that were up and down his arms, and Andy turned to his too. They scratched without thinking, the flaky skin growing redder and angrier with each passing moment.

A stranger touching Chrissy was strictly no-go, so when the young photographer touched him lightly in an attempt to reposition him for the photo, his body immediately tensed up. Andy, seeing this, but not wanting to chastise him in front of the extended family, whispered a harsh warning. Dad asked Andy to calm down. Andy took to his skin like sandpaper. It began to bleed. Chrissy's innocent eyes filled with tears.

'Smile!' said the photographer.

The moment was captured forever and would be hung on our grandmother's wall like a prize. I remember looking out into the camera and smiling, but aware of my cousins around me: no one else was having anything like a stressful reaction.

Why should they? It was just a photo.

This is the first moment I can remember being properly furious with my family. The boys were exhausted and quiet on the drive back. But now I was the one who wanted to take to the interior of the car and scratch at it red raw.

'Why couldn't you be normal?' I snapped at them.

Dad interrupted before the boys could respond. 'It's all right, it's all over now.'

But it wasn't over. This was my family for the rest of my life, and the boys couldn't even take a photo. I wanted to scream at how unfair my life was.

Mum tried to calm me down.

'I know it's hard,' she said. 'But you've just got to accept it. They are the way they are.'

I began an extended campaign to prove them wrong.

∿∿∿

While I was trying to survive my personal high-school ordeal, the boys were trying to survive theirs.

Primary school had been tolerable for them for a couple of reasons. One was the tiny size of the country school, where all manner of eccentricities were accepted and embraced. Another was the fact that my father was their teacher for their final years there.

A student's success at primary school is softly measured. Children are measured against themselves: how far they've come from where they were, whether they're in danger of falling back. Once you hit secondary school, you're clearly told that the time of being a child is over. Success is now measured by the distance between you and that of an acceptably functioning adult. So, the boys went directly from an environment where their own pace of progress was applauded to one where they were destined to fail.

My brothers attended a large public high school on the other side of town from mine. It was reputed to have the best special-education unit in the state.

It's difficult to imagine that first day for the twins. I was in year ten at the time, at the zenith of my complications with Mary.

There would have been noise. A lot of it. It would have been amplified in their ears, a constant hum of anxiety. Buildings in all directions, jammed full of teenagers—laughing, pushing and cajoling each other. Andy and Chrissy would have been led by the hand to the special-education unit, a beautifully equipped room, recently refurbished.

Inside, a chaotic mix of strangers awaited them. Students in wheelchairs, their limbs hanging limply and their faces resting on their shoulders, their shirts collecting drool. Another few yelling and swearing at the top of their lungs, trying desperately to overpower the mild-mannered, middle-aged women who were trying to manage them. The silent. The meek. The frustrated. The terminally ill. The boys were brought to this room and told, 'You belong here'.

Chrissy's soul would've curled up and tucked itself

away somewhere inside, hiding in deep fear. Andy would've breathed in, puffed his chest outwards. He would make it his personal mission to be normal, even if it killed him.

Chrissy's time at the high school was brief and rarely pleasant. The wonderfully kind, gently innocent individual we all knew and loved was threatening to disappear forever. Under the strain of adolescence and the cacophony of high school, Chrissy was becoming someone else. He would resort to the only language he knew to explain it: the dialogue of Spider-man's Venom, or *Pokémon's* MewTwo, or a 'very naughty engine' from *Thomas the Tank Engine*. Within a few short months, the Chrissy that would never hurt a fly turned angry and dark. He yelled at teachers, scratched his arms raw, and threw punches at desks and chairs. He had an escape valve: a walk around the oval.

While I'm sitting in a boring lesson, in between trying to figure out if Christine Pennyworth likes me and what I can do to make Mary laugh, my mind turns to imagining what Chrissy's doing at that precise moment. I see him in the peace of a school oval. The sky is enormous and blue and stretches far above him. He surrenders to it, lost in the endlessness of it. The school, with its noise and nonsense, is miles away, a small collection of buildings in the distance. It can't bother him out here.

I imagine I'm walking beside him. I'm envious of his escape route. I look up into the sky with him and wonder if he can see more than me. Maybe he sees beyond the blue, into the black, into the stars and planets that circle around him, letting him play with them in a ceaseless cosmic dance that calms him down.

I imagine him feeling the gentle tap on the shoulder from his teacher. It's time to go back inside. His heart breaks. But, because he doesn't want to let his family down, he turns around and follows his teacher back inside, back to his own personal hell.

When the time on the oval became greater than the time he spent in the classroom, the futility of the exercise was apparent. Chrissy assumed a part-time enrolment that gradually shrank smaller and smaller. By the end of year nine, he was out of school completely.

Andy lasted longer out of sheer will and determination. He went to normal classes with the assistance of a teacher's aide, but he often asked to step outside. The sheer volume of noise and the other students' apparent inability to listen to the teacher and follow very logical instructions completely stressed him out. High school should be a logical place. A teacher tells you something. You do it. Done. Andy couldn't accept the huge number of variables within this simple equation. Worse, he was told, implicitly, that these students were 'normal' and he was the 'special' one.

Of course, Andy was an easy target for vicious and unintelligent bullies, who would degrade him with the usual litany of insults that the terminally stupid always seem to reach for: gay, faggot, cock head, etc. He would come home speaking of his 'nemesis'. Seen through the lens of his pop-culture glasses, high school was a battle-ground, and he was the hero, striding forth to survive in a world that was up against him.

Andy made it his personal goal to get to the end of year ten. He made it, but the effort left him exhausted. His skin was raw, and he was almost permanently set against the human race.

Mum, Dad and I were proud of him and of Chrissy for how long they'd managed to tough it out. But I was a loud (and probably annoying) voice in my parents' discussions about the boys. Mum and Dad constantly wrestled with the question: how far do we push them? How much do we let them rest? Usually, Dad would lean towards the gentler option. I would lean to the more aggressive side. Mum would be somewhere in the middle.

Part of my behaviour was motivated by jealousy. In fact, a lot of it was jealousy. I had lost so many hours of my life, strapped to a school desk trying to find a way to tolerate and accept the chaos that was happening around me. I'd never once had the option to escape to the school oval for a breather, or to work with a personal assistant to receive my education at my own pace. Mum and Dad had done all they could. They talked with my teachers about bumping me up to classes that were above my year in order to keep me engaged and challenged. They even offered me the same deal they gave to the boys: get out; be homeschooled.

I didn't see that as an option; I wanted to be normal more than anything. So I was destined to be unhappy no matter what I did. If I fell out of school, I was a failure, and I resented that I had to figure it out while the boys received a special pass. To be honest, it infuriated me.

This wasn't to say that I didn't regard the boys as special cases, or that I dismissed their very real disability. A big part of me wanted to protect them, to go to their school and fix it for them. This is the contradiction in all families, I guess: that thing that will drive you bonkers if you let it. It's a feat of emotional quantum trickery: you simultaneously feel protective, loving and loyal to your family, as much as you do infuriated, resentful and bitter about them. And that's not to mention the incessant *guilt* that you feel for being infuriated, resentful or bitter about them.

Underneath all of this I had a deep concern for my parents. Dad was rapidly running out of energy for his teaching career. Mum was under attack from frequent migraines, lost in her own battles between motherhood and career. Both in difficult places and under a lot of pressure, Mum and Dad saw a number of psychologists and psychiatrists who had prescribed them antidepressants for years. The boys, facing their own anxieties, were also given medication. For all of my adolescence, I was the only family member not on antidepressants. Even our dog, bound in neurosis and skin itches, had a pill hidden in her breakfast each morning.

This point of difference wasn't for lack of trying on my parents' part. There were many times when they thought medication would help me, and they held a continual campaign to get me to go and see a psychologist. But I wasn't concerned about my mental state; I was more worried about them. With my entire family medicated and stressed out, I feared they would detach from the world and lose their way, and perhaps take me with them.

With militant zeal, I took on the task of making sure this didn't happen. I wanted a family that could take a goddam picture. I wanted a family that didn't start its day with a conveyor belt of pills. I wanted a family that went on holidays and did things. I wanted a family who didn't celebrate special occasions by going out to Sizzler. Every. Goddam. Time. (Chrissy is a big fan of the spaghetti. It's one of the only things he'll eat out. Sizzler spaghetti.)

It was difficult for Mum and Dad to register this

effort of mine as anything other than shame for the way our family operated, and they responded with a complex range of emotions. Part of them wanted me to be afforded the opportunities that many other kids in my position had, so they reacted to things like the Rachel and New Zealand trip with absolute glee, stained with guilt for not being able to provide such an experience themselves.

My frustration with them often surfaced as irritability. I took on the role of cultural snob in many of my interactions with them, to which they responded in kind. Whenever I talked proudly of my drama degree, elements of which they would happily admit they didn't understand, they would often dismiss my passion with laughter, warning me not to turn into a high-falutin' arty farter. This game of making all of us feel bad about ourselves created no winners, but it soon became a habit.

Already confused and suffering from anxiety around my sexuality, career and general human worth in the world, I now added an unhealthy mental dialogue about my family, which was no assistance whatsoever.

This tightly wound nest of intense emotions festered over many years. It's amazing how long negativity can sustain itself. During that difficult time, with schooling, retirement, depression and anxiety all happening concurrently, we all suffered.

Something had to give.

In the second year of uni, I made the seemingly 'normal' decision to move out of home. It caused enough of a schism in my family to threaten to tear us apart for good.

On the day after I moved out, my mother was on the phone, angrier than almost any other time I had heard her. Several weeks ago, I had given a copy of a DVD to a uni friend, who was yet to return it. Mum wanted to lend it to one of her friends.

'This is so like you,' she said. 'Selfish. Putting your friends before your family. Your friends before mine. As if your friends are more important.'

We swapped sharp words for many minutes before I finally said: 'Mum, are you upset about the DVD? Or are you upset that I've moved out of home?'

Silence.

'Well,' she said eventually, still furious, 'it's true, isn't it? You put your friends before us.'

There was little I could say in response. Yes, right now I was putting my friends before my family. It felt like the right thing to do. I was a nineteen-year-old student.

The conversation fizzled, and I told her I'd get the DVD back to her as soon as I could. I hung up the phone. I had no idea how to have a relationship with my family that didn't involve me living with them. Maybe I was selfish. Maybe I should have stayed at home for longer.

It soon became clear that my choice of roommates was not ideal. I moved into a house with Ravi and Rachel, and the household turned out to be about as functional as you'd expect it to be, with each of us confused about who or what we wanted.

On our first night in our new home, and my first night away from my family, we discovered our landlord had left two cases of pre-mixed vodka in the run-down fridge in the garage. We took to it with gusto. After a lengthy night of drinking, we stumbled to bed. My bedroom was not yet set up, so I climbed into Rachel's, where I promptly projectile-vomited all over her very expensive mattress and pink-frilled doona. While the translucent poison of the alcohol came bursting from my nose and mouth in great gushing spurts, I had a brief thought: maybe the whole not-living-with-my-family thing won't work out quite the way I was expecting.

Our house had an enormous yard, and it became the party rendezvous for the entire university arts faculty. After my initial flirtation with parties, they had lost their novelty. They had gone back to causing me anxiety. I felt out of place. I just wanted to watch television quietly and go to bed.

Two nights after I moved in, the house was filled with drunk, noisy theatre students. After several hours of pretending to enjoy myself, I slipped away quietly to my room. It was after midnight; I needed to sleep. When I switched on the light, I found two of my classmates, half-naked and making out, on my bed. I switched off the light and left them to it.

I drove back to my family home. I still had keys. The house was sweetly silent. I curled up on the couch in the living room and fell asleep instantly.

The next morning, I snuck out before anyone saw me.

∿∿∿

I moved in with Amber a couple of months later.

The decision to live with Amber turned out to be a stroke of genius. My friendship with Amber was pretty much my first healthy friendship with a female ever. I found in her something I had found nowhere else: laughter, safety and mutual respect. After years of searching, out of nowhere, and without really looking, I had found the positive female friendship that I'd always wanted.

With Amber, I finally started to come home. The person I found when I walked through our front door, in our small (but tidier than average) uni flat, was supportive and welcoming. Beside her, I would find myself to be a generous and likeable young man. I sat with long limbs at odd angles, laughing with her on the couch and sipping a beer, about to enter the fifth consecutive hour of television, relaxed and smiling. I was quietly astounded. It was a version of myself that I had never known. I was a stranger to myself.

I was me. But I was happy.

I hadn't realised it before, but I had been lonely for most of my life. I had been too wound up in anxiety and negativity to truly connect with anyone. Running away from myself, from friendships, from my family, had left me alone and locked inside my own head for a long time. I thought I had had good friends, but my relationships had been so laden with other circumstances that I had never allowed them to grow into true friendships.

'I have an exam tomorrow,' Amber sighs.

'You deserve a break,' I say. 'I'm putting a *Friends* DVD in.'

'Good. Right. Where's the remote?'

'I've got it.'

'Can you hit "play all", please, David?'

'But what about your exam?'

'Play. All.'

Across town, our fellow students were having a party. We were watching *Friends* and laughing and asleep by ten. It was perfect.

But my mind wrestled with guilt. Perhaps it was selfish to seek such comfort. It was certainly disrespectful to be openly disdainful of my family. I'm still not sure what a child owes their parents once they grow up, or vice versa. In a period of your life where everything is about choice (your friends, your mode of study, your living arrangements) it's difficult to give your family the respect they deserve. There's a lot of other things going on.

I didn't realise I was hurting people in quite a profound way, purely because I didn't have the courage to turn around and examine my actions properly.

I had played recklessly with Rachel's heart.

I had not given my parents the acknowledgment they were due. They had both made every effort to make me happy. This included attempting to combat my depressive nature with numerous doctors' visits. I hadn't let them.

Truth was, I didn't stop to reflect or really talk about my family with anyone, least of all myself. My stance was clear. I was growing up, I was no longer in need of my family, and I was desperately independent. This distance I put between us felt good as I dived head-first into my university years. I drank, smoked pot, and lived a carefree uni-student life. I thought I was unstoppable.

I would come to regret my silence. In the months to come, my inability to face how I was actually feeling would cause me to attempt to end my own life.

I was nowhere near done growing up.

15

Turning Inside Out

With my single night with James as my one gay sex experience, and still secretly suffering massive confusion over my sexuality, I did the only sensible thing I could. I appointed myself the town's young leader on gay rights.

Any time the government talked about its opposition to gay marriage or adoption, I appeared in the paper claiming outrage. I wrote furiously on the issue of inequality, calling out for social justice. I was angry and determined. I spoke with confidence. I was Gay Dave, and I was proud.

My lack of sexual experience didn't bother me.

Seriously. I had kissed a guy. That made me Captain Gay.

I put my celibacy down to nerves. I was privately sure that one day I would summon the courage to go cruising and pick up a beautiful man. I bored Amber to death with my endless list of longings and crushes. I was still desperate for romantic intimacy, but I did little about it. The thought of approaching an actual person and flirting caused my body to shake with fear. I would find myself saying all the wrong things in front of even the most mildly attractive of men, and then I would relive my dorkiness a thousand times in my head, letting myself almost reach a panic attack before I tried to calm myself.

I made a lot of external noise to compensate for my inner turmoil. My final project as an undergraduate is a perfect example.

It started out simply enough. I would interview a bunch of parents and grown children about homosexuality, combining the material into a short play, the draft of which I would deliver to my lecturers, and it would be read aloud to my classmates. This seemed entirely suitable to Donna, although she was a little concerned that I had set myself too much work. I scoffed. I would be fine. Besides, this town needed a play like this. I was Gay Dave, after all, and it was my responsibility to lead the cause.

I had a brief meeting with a gay-health organisation in Brisbane. They applauded the project's philosophy and happily donated three hundred dollars as sponsorship.

Three hundred dollars.

That was a budget.

This was a proper project now.

With that kind of money, I did what any gay-rights leader would do: I trashed the idea of a reading and decided to put on a full production. I would have a cast. They would have costumes. There would be a set.

But only one show? No. Three shows. And then another two shows in Brisbane. Yes. A touring production.

I would write, produce and direct the show.

Too much work?

Pffft.

I had never directed or produced anything before. Luckily, I was Gay Dave, and gay people do theatre. It's one of their superpowers. So I wasn't worried.

Make no mistake, the show was awful. But what it lacked in craft, experience, knowledge or narrative cohesion, it made up for in enthusiasm. I was ticking two major boxes. The first was, of course, being Gay Dave, inspirational leader to the under-experienced and confused. When people saw this play, they would say things like:

'Hey, gay people are all right.' 'I was gonna bash a faggot, but now I'm not going to.' 'Man, I think I've been feeling gay, but I've been too scared to admit it. I'm going to go out and get a sweet dickin'.'

All of this because of me.

The second box I ticked was putting on a play, and I had figured out that that was what I really wanted to do. More than act, I wanted to write plays. So off I went to assemble a cast.

I asked my friends. Nina jumped in, although not without rolling her eyes at my 'poetry'.

'"The whole world is inside me, and it's ending",' she read from her script. She looked up to me. 'Really?'

I nodded enthusiastically. 'Yeah. She's having an orgasm.'

'So,' she began, with slight confusion, 'she's not enjoying it?'

'No! It's brilliant! It's her first truly liberated moment.'

'Right. But it feels like the apocalypse?'

'It's beautiful.'

'Yeah, it sure is, Dave,' she said with a smirk. 'It sure is.'

I was proud of that scene, where all four characters (two male, two female, all gay) described these beautiful sexual experiences. It was rendered as pure romance, and it was completely fake. Because, after all,

I had almost no experience of a beautiful sexual experience. Nina persistently challenged me on my bullshit, but my facade was so thick at this point that her subtle protests bounced off with barely a whimper.

But with Nina's assistance and one particularly helpful and intense rehearsal with Donna, more than a third of my material was cut and replaced. The show went on. My mum drove the cast to the performances. My parents and extended family happily attended.

Picture my sweet grandmother at an art gallery that held a dozen people in inner-north Brisbane, as a small cast yells in her face about the woes of being gay and young. She beamed with pride for me the entire time.

'Wonderful!' she said, hugging me after the show.

Nina's lesbian partner in the play was a girl called Dani, a free-spirited teacher-in-training whom I had met through a friend of a friend. She took to the show enthusiastically, and gave a gorgeous performance of my flaccid script.

We topped off the season with an afterparty, the spirit of which reflected the afterparty where I had first played spin the bottle three years earlier. Gay Dave was happy. He had fulfilled his mission.

Gay Dave got very drunk and made out with Dani for quite some time in a private corner of the backyard.

Gay Dave. An experienced, confident campaigner for homosexual rights.

As if we were living a badly written sitcom, Dani and I began seeing each other in secret. If we didn't tell other people, we wouldn't have to admit it to ourselves. Dani wasn't too keen to broadcast the news that she was fooling around with a gay guy. We both had reasons to keep it quiet.

Dani was short, wide-eyed, and had long strawberry-blonde hair. She was gorgeous—there was no use denying it. But it was her attitude and spirit that I was attracted to. Dani was laid-back. About everything. There was very little in life that Dani felt warranted being worried or stressed over. She was drifting through a teaching degree, but she found herself hanging out with theatre people.

Happiness came easy to Dani. Where I thought, talked, analysed, planned and worried, Dani laughed. Life was easy. Life was a game. The energy of it was irresistible to me. Her level of chaos was just the right salve for my tightly bound soul.

Besides, the physical affection was fun. And, for the time being, it appeared to come with no strings attached. It also happened slowly. Clothes tended to stay on. It was gentle. It was sneaky.

Amber was the only one who knew, and she'd just roll her eyes when she came home from uni to find

Dani and me on the couch—again. Amber shrugged about the entire relationship, but I could tell she had her doubts.

'Have fun,' she said. 'But be careful.'

I wasn't sure what I needed to be careful of. All I could feel was the blissful freefall.

I felt relieved. I felt like a balloon that had been close to bursting, my skin stretched tight and void of colour, now finally exhaled, loose and full of potential once again.

Dani, somehow, understood. Perhaps not with her head but certainly with her heart. I don't know what I gave her in those months. I couldn't tell you why she stayed. But her affection spurred mine on, and the relationship gained momentum. It was growing out of my control. We met more and more often, and I found myself thinking about her constantly.

I soon felt the familiar sting of fear. What if this fling was not yet flung? What if Dani and I actually began a relationship?

But the question had a convenient point of resolution. I was moving to Brisbane soon, with Amber. Uni was finishing and my untidy life was being packed into my even untidier hatchback. Dani was finishing her degree too, but I drew a clear line.

We would not continue after I moved.

I wasn't sure what I wanted, but the move felt like

an appropriate point for me to withdraw and reassess.

And so I was to drop Dani at her parents' house for the Christmas holidays, and then continue, with my final load of boxes, to my new house in Brisbane. By my own rules, it was to be the last time Dani and I would see each other.

I had also created other neat little rules. While our layers of clothing had gradually come off, my virginity was still very much intact. That was a threshold that I was not prepared to trip over.

I was gay. Right?

I had spent the last three years building an identity based on my sexuality. To have it demolished would be disastrous.

Who was I if I wasn't Gay Dave? Just 'Dave'? What did that even mean?!

Crazy Drama Dave was long dead, and Gay Dave was facing death threats from a free-spirited hippie woman. I couldn't allow this to happen. I had rules. Dani and I would end. And I would find Gay Dave alive and well in Brisbane.

The only issue was we were sharing a car for the final trip. And it was raining. Loading the last of my boxes had left us both soaking wet. We rushed into the car, our clothes squelching. The windows instantly fogged up. We both shed a few layers.

Suddenly, the car seemed very small. And Dani

seemed very close. And my heart seemed to be beating very fast.

I started the car.

It was a ninety-minute drive. Just ninety minutes. That's all I had to do. Just turn the music up and get us to Brisbane, wave her goodbye, maybe a quick kiss, and then I would go back to being the person I knew how to be.

Dani had other ideas.

And, to be honest, so did I.

'Turn here,' she said. We were only a few minutes from her parents' place. 'And here,' she said again.

We were driving away from houses, towards a park.

'Stop here,' she said, and she got out of the car. She flew her hands open, welcoming the rain.

I followed her.

Around us, the trees and grass glistened a clean and shiny green. Our lips met, cold and slippery.

We found ourselves in the back of the car. It happened quickly. We still had most of our clothes on. We made a brief, clumsy attempt to find condoms. There were none.

But it happened.

My mind went into white noise.

I couldn't think, or even feel, I was absent, forcing my eyes away from hers, facing elsewhere, immersing my head into nothing. I wanted it to happen, but my body was filled with anxiety.

It was over within a minute.

I was no longer a virgin.

The air seemed to vanish out of the car. I wasn't sure if Dani was pleased, or disappointed, or perhaps as confused as I was. We sat in silence, the rain hammering gently on the car roof.

'I should take you home,' I said.

She nodded and smiled gently. 'Yeah,' she said.

I dropped her off at her parents' place and drove to Amber and our neat little Brisbane home.

It should've been that simple, I suppose. Some part of my brain was certain that we would never see each other again.

Except we hadn't used protection.

16

Lost and Found

And now I couldn't get that thought out of my mind.

We hadn't used protection.

I suppose I had thought of it in the middle of it all. I was too afraid, too filled with every emotion on the planet, to stop and actually think. I didn't want to be crap, I didn't want to disappoint her, I didn't want to... *not* have sex.

Dammit. I had wanted it. Somehow. Weirdly.

I didn't sleep that night. And I rang Dani the next morning.

'You're thinking too much,' she said. I could hear her smile over the phone.

My mind couldn't let it go. I asked her if she'd take the morning-after pill.

There was a long silence.

I said, 'I'll buy it, I'll bring it over, whatever. I'd just really like you to take it.'

Another pause. A sigh. 'Yeah, okay,' she said, 'I'll take it if it makes you feel better.'

This was a girl I'd planned on saying goodbye to only twelve hours earlier. Now I was calling her, embarrassed, asking her to take something that would have a huge effect on her body.

It wasn't one of my greatest moments.

That afternoon I turned up at Dani's place with the foil packet in my hand. I left it in a pot plant by the side of her house, and I texted her when I was driving away. You know, because I was being really brave about it.

I couldn't sleep again that night. It was nearly midnight. I was watching TV. In the dark, I saw the shape of her car pull up. She came to the door.

'I need food to take it,' she said. 'I need food.'

I found an apple and gave it to her. I got a glass, filled it with water, and put it in her hand.

'Thank you,' I said, as she put the tiny thing into her mouth and swallowed it, chasing it with water.

That was it, apparently. It was done now.

She'd really taken it. It was over.

I walked her outside, down our dusty driveway. We hugged goodbye, and she got in the car.

'I'll see you around, Dave,' she said.

She turned the key.

Nothing happened.

Again.

A faint, whining murmur from the car. And then nothing.

Her car was stuffed.

One awkward call to RACQ later, we were sitting on the bonnet of her car, staring up into the stars.

The air was mild. It was a Brisbane summer: the days were unbearably hot and the evenings pleasantly still. Our busy suburban street was stone quiet.

'It's all a bit sad, isn't it?' I said.

'What?'

'The pill. The whole thing. It's just...quick.'

I wasn't sure what I was saying. Or thinking. Suddenly life was unreal. Had I just killed something? And with Gay Dave gone, who was I?

'Did you *want* me to be pregnant?' she asked. I didn't know how to answer the question.

'No,' I said, 'I don't think so.'

Yes, I'd thought about it. A future with a child and Dani by my side. Some grand vision where I could be straight, happy and live a 'normal' life. I'd finally be a normal guy. My old dream came echoing back to me.

But somehow life wasn't that simple anymore.

'It's just funny what doors you end up closing,' I said, quietly. I knew I probably wasn't making any sense. 'Are you angry at me?'

She was silent for a moment. 'No. Well, yes. I think I'm just hurt. I don't know. You worry a lot, Dave. You think way too much. And I think I've caught it off you.'

I really liked Dani. I realised that as I was staring up at the stars, with the cold deadness of the car underneath me. I really liked her. But being with Dani meant I wasn't the man I thought I was. Only twelve hours ago I'd hopped in the car intending to drive away from this confusing relationship and start anew. And I think Dani knew that.

'I'm sorry,' I said, but it felt feeble.

A yellow RACQ ute came rolling up the street.

We pretended to be a happy couple for a minute for the sake of the mechanic. The car rumbled to life easily with a quick heart start to the battery, and the yellow ute disappeared down the street. Dani got back in the car.

It was over. Again.

As easily as a gulp of water, or a quick kiss in the rain, or a question without an answer hanging in the still night, Dani drove off.

Apparently, I had my wish fulfilled.

It was three years since I had come out to my family, and I was spinning out of control. I was miserable. I'd let a perfectly good relationship slip away because of my clumsiness. Yet again, I'd managed to hurt the feelings of a woman I really cared about.

Was I gay? Straight? Who the hell was I? Being unemployed in the big bad city didn't help. My relationship with my family was distant and I had nobody to blame but myself. But I kept pushing them away.

I was exhausted. It felt as if I had been running for years. Dani was right, I spent *way* too much time thinking, and it had only ever gotten me into trouble. Gay Dave was a lie. I had made a complete fool of myself. Captain Gay? I felt as if I had let my community down. I'd been with a girl.

After all this time, I'd finally had sex. But it hadn't been the pleasing rush of romance that I had expected. It hadn't fulfilled me.

Suddenly, my life looked very different. I had very little. I became lost in my own mind, disappearing quickly into darkness. I felt a despairing void open up and take me in.

I was so tired of running. So tired of constantly feeling like I wasn't good enough. I hated being this needy, weak, pathetic little man. How sweet it would be to not have this pain anymore. How easy and light would my soul be, if freed from this constant trouble?

From the void, a seductive question came. It crept up so slowly it seemed nothing less than normal.

What if I died?

Familiar dark daydreams came back to me. I could see it, clear as anything: my own body, pleasingly crushed under the weight of six feet of soil resting heavily on my chest. I would lie there in the warm wet darkness, gradually losing air, feeling my brain slowly loosen its tight and worried grip on reality, and I would pass. Like air. Like nothing.

It seemed a sensible solution.

I didn't dare say a word to anyone. If I asked for help it would only cause people concern, and I didn't want any attention on me. I wasn't worth a second glance, and, besides, telling people would mean questions that I didn't want to answer. Questions like: 'What do you mean you're not gay?' or 'How could you treat all of those women like that? They wanted to kill themselves because of you!' and 'You've really fucked a lot of people over, haven't you?'

Even my relationship with Amber, something that felt robust, suddenly seemed under threat. I hadn't told her about the morning-after pill and sex episode. Amber had grown increasingly silent on the subject of Dani. Amber, a beautifully grounded being, didn't trust

Dani's free-spirited energy to take care of my fragile heart. If I told Amber what was happening, I would have to admit that I had real feelings for Dani. The idea of admitting that to Amber caused my brain to go into overdrive. I was sure I would lose my best friend.

But I couldn't get my mind off Dani. Dreams and thoughts persisted. The images of death and dying increased. I began to fear washing the dishes. I didn't trust myself with the knives. I kept seeing their naked steely allure underneath a pile of soapy bubbles. How easy it would be to clutch my hand around one...swear it was a mistake...let the dark red blood ribbon out into the warm water.

I stood at the sink one afternoon, realising I had been thinking about this for some time. The window above the sink faced onto the neighbours' backyard. They hadn't mown their grass in months. Dry and yellow, it almost looked, absurdly, like a field of wheat. The wind moved it gently, and the blades swayed as one. It was staggeringly beautiful, and the surreal moment of clarity brought tears to my eyes. I sobbed on the kitchen floor for three hours.

Then I finished the dishes, had a shower and carried on as normal, welcoming Amber home when she walked through the door.

I felt as if I had given up a romantic relationship before it had even begun. I needed to be with Dani. The conversation we had around her broken-down car kept playing over in my mind. It was suddenly so obvious. I should never have let her drive away.

I messaged Dani and we arranged to meet for coffee. She told me about her new boyfriend. I put on my best happy face. This beautiful new man was tall, muscular and tanned from the outdoors. He was unworried about life, and apparently as relaxed and carefree as she was. They had such fun together, she said.

I hugged her goodbye. We laughed. And I got back in the car.

I had visions of my car in a field, my own corpse, cold and pale inside it. Or my body lying face down in long grass, the wind gently caressing my back, the warm earth against my chest, a stab wound in my heart from a knife that I hold loosely in my outstretched hand.

I make a plan. I will go back home and get pills. And a knife. I will drive somewhere and come to a brutal and quick end. I will lie in my own field of wheat, and feel myself vanish into the earth. I will be free. Finally.

I pull up and I curse when I see Amber's car in the driveway. This will call for stealth. I will have to grab pills discreetly and go straight back to the car. In and out. Don't answer any questions. Just go.

I get out of the car and catch something in the corner of my eye. On my messy back seat is a scrap of paper with a phone number. I had written it down months ago, when I asked Mum for my old psychologist's number. I had been planning on calling him for research for an upcoming play. It was Gary's number.

I found myself picking it up and calling him from the driveway.

The number went to voicemail.

'Hi,' I said. 'Gary? I think I need help.'

He called me back a short time later, and we booked an appointment for the following week.

I had stopped seeing Gary shortly after I started at university. I hadn't really considered talking to Gary as an option before I saw the phone number on my car's back seat. The promise of an appointment was a promise to stay alive, but I was scared to go and talk to him.

I found talking about my inner state incredibly difficult, especially with those closest to me. I was too scared to tell Amber that I was feeling uncontrollably sad and miserable because I didn't want to let her down. I didn't want to tell my family that I was feeling awful because I didn't want to prove that their continual attempts to help me were in fact incredibly well founded. I kept myself in misery for months purely to avoid confronting them.

I had strict stiff-upper-lip syndrome. I kept a smile

on my face. I hoped that if I persisted with this for long enough, I would quash the intense feelings of despair that were threatening to end my life. I reached for alcohol and pot to help the repression. But the void only became larger. And I became further lost within it.

So why the defence? What's so terrifying about therapy? The truth is that therapy can be scary.

Therapy is a mirror. It's a reflective surface that your inner-state bounces off. You go in, sit down, and look at yourself head on.

For someone who doesn't consider themselves worthy of walking the earth, this is like looking into the eyes of Satan himself. Make no mistake, I thought I was unlovable. I believed I had evidence to prove my point. I had covered who I was with a great performance for many years. Now, without Crazy Drama Dave or Gay Dave to lean upon, I was left the raw shell of a sad human being. Inside that shell was a dark void, containing one very small, very unhappy, very ugly human being. Why would I want to go to someone and pay them for helping me look at that?

To heal a broken arm, you have to examine the broken arm. You have to X-ray it, diagnose it and tell the story of how it got hurt. You can't stick a cast on it and hope for the best. It may heal incorrectly, always carrying the cracks of the injury in its structure. I wouldn't have been ashamed of doing all of that to get my arm fixed. Why did I feel that way about my brain?

In my sessions with Gary, I was undergoing a form of Cognitive Behavioural Therapy, or CBT. In CBT, the psychologist assists you with navigating your thoughts and emotions by helping you see the behaviour of your thoughts and how it affects you. This means, as I said, they will often act as a mirror, asking questions designed to help you dig deeper into your state of mind.

And that can be a scary and challenging place to be. It's easy to be in denial, even in therapy. It's easy to go in, figure out the game (CBT), and never be truly emotionally open.

I was a mess by the time I got back to Gary. I slowly began to unload some of my worries. I was uncomfortable, but I was now too drained to feel anything properly. The thoughts of darkness kept any emotion at bay. Happiness, anger, passion—they all felt like memories I had lost long ago.

Gary outlined a six-week plan.

I wish I could say I went to those sessions with Gary and really came to terms with who I was. I took the time to slowly unpack what was going on inside my own head and the reasons for my continually self-destructive behaviour.

But I couldn't see past Dani. I was sad because I

had lost a relationship. It was a relationship I hadn't expected, with a gender I didn't believe I was aroused by, and it left me bewildered. That much I was willing to admit. Gary helped me to work through those thoughts.

If I truly believed sexuality was fluid, and there was life beyond the straight/gay dichotomy, then what did it matter if I found a woman attractive? And wouldn't my family and friends understand that?

'You need to tell people what's going on,' Gary advised. 'You need to get better at that. Tell someone.'

I told Amber. I told her I was going to see Gary and that I'd been confused and deeply sad for many months.

'You didn't tell me,' she said.

Her lips grew tight and she took a few sharp breaths.

I told her about the washing up. About the tears. And about the thought of suicide. I posed it as a joke. 'You won't believe what I nearly did...', as if it was a drunken night out. I laughed.

Amber didn't think it was funny. In fact, she walked away into her bedroom and closed the door.

She was warm and friendly again by that afternoon, but we didn't discuss it after that. She kept her older-sister eye on me, and I let her. Besides, things were starting to get better.

I kept talking to Dani. I rang her and we'd talk for hours.

'How's the new boyfriend?' I'd ask.

Silence for a moment, before, 'Good. Good.'

'I'm glad. That's really good.'

And then she'd come round and we'd find ourselves on the bed or the couch, just holding each other. It felt warm. It felt loving.

'I shouldn't be holding you like this,' I said to her.

'Why not?'

'Your boyfriend.'

She got up and made a cup of tea. 'You're right.'

Within minutes she had collapsed into my arms again.

Our attempt at being 'just friends' seemed to be impossible. I was undeniably attracted to her. And she was attracted to me. I was secretly hoping she would break it off with the new man.

I needed advice.

'What do you think I should do?' I asked Amber.

Once again her lips tightened. 'If you really think, *really* think, that Dani will make you happier and make life easier, then go for it. But you should really think about that. Because if it ends, however it ends, you don't want to end up in the same place again.'

I asked Gary the same question.

'Well, what do you think you should do?' he asked in return.

Clever bastard.

It was my third or fourth session. I didn't go back after that.

Gutless Wonder

'Mum, Dad, I need to tell you something. It might make you mad, and perhaps you have a right to be. I don't know. I don't know anymore. I'm seeing someone. It's a woman.'

There's a second's pause, and then laughter. From both of them. Mum rolls her eyes.

'Whatever, Dave. Whatever you think.'

Dad seems slightly disappointed. 'But you would've been proud of me Dave. I've been getting my head round it. The other day I saw this guy and I thought: Dave might like him.'

Once again the consequences of my confession had

proven far less cataclysmic than I had imagined them to be. I had built up this conversation for days in my head, convinced that my parents would be furious for my seemingly unending confusion. Quite to the contrary, they weren't upset at all.

My initial embarrassment about 'coming in' to my friends and family was soon overshadowed by my renewed affair with Dani.

'Something's got to give,' I said to her. 'We can't keep on like this.'

'Well what are we supposed to do? I still want to hang out with you, Dave.'

'The only way that can happen, I think, is if you're not seeing someone else. It's not fair to him that you and I are spending so much time together.'

Within a few days, Dani had broken it off with her boyfriend.

There was no turning back now. We leapt into the full velocity of each other without hesitation. It was a giddy, dizzying fall.

Just like that, everything was fixed.

Weeks passed, each one feeling like a milestone. Dani had never had a relationship longer than a couple of months, so when we got to nine weeks it felt as though we had achieved something. A truly happy, committed relationship. I celebrated by doing my best to disappear inside Dani's personality and make her every whim come true.

Dani made me incessantly happy. I uncovered positive emotions in myself that I had never encountered before. With Dani, life felt lighter. Her biggest criticism of me was only that I thought too much, and she did her best to shake me out of my own brain. It was a welcome shift. I fell in love with Dani's relaxed and carefree lifestyle.

But I suspected I was in danger. Carefree? Relaxed? My idea of a long, serious, committed relationship didn't fit that description. Anytime I brought up bigger talk of the future, Dani became very quiet. I sensed I was playing a delicate game. If I wasn't careful, my over-analysing would push Dani away. In so many ways we were very unlike each other. So I set about changing myself to eliminate these differences so that we could have a long and happy partnership.

I attempted to embrace a hippy and carefree attitude. I wore fishermen's pants and tie-dyed T-shirts. I attended parties with her and convinced myself that I was a secret extrovert. I did everything I could to quiet the part of my brain that wanted to know about the future and where this relationship would be going.

After all, the concept of losing Dani was too terrifying to contemplate. So why contemplate it? If I was smart and made her happy, there would be no need to ever consider a life without her.

I had ideas about how long-term relationships operated. These ideas were based on movies, mostly, and other successful relationships I had observed. They required devotion and commitment. They required compromise and change. So I once again became a different version of myself. I was Dani's loveable boyfriend. I was so laid-back I was almost falling over.

Dani took to the notion of having a career with the force of a gentle breeze. Graduating from teaching, she moved on to do a certificate in dressmaking, before contemplating visual arts, and then nursing, all the while cafe-hopping as a waitress. I struggled with this casual approach to her professional life, but I began to take to my own job prospects with a certain amount of indifference, and I stopped myself from thinking about my career future.

We committed, career-wise, to drifting. That is, we committed to not committing.

Dani was very social and incredibly extroverted. She'd come home from a party energised, where I'd end up feeling drained. This strain of introversion was one I really struggled to shift, and it became our greatest point of tension. I did my best to join her and her friends for long nights of drinks, music and mad conversations, but it wore thin pretty quickly. Equally, for Dani, cosy nights in front of the television were about as invigorating as a visit to the local funeral home. We each tried to accommodate the other, mis-moulding our personalities in the process.

Dani did have one specific vision. One grand life goal. It was simple, but it was real. Buy a van, use it as a home, and travel around Australia.

It was a goal that I thought could keep us together. I came up with a plan.

In a few months, my lease on the house with Amber would be up. Dani and I would spend those months saving, then we'd purchase a van and take to the wide open road.

That was, literally, the entire plan. It was short on detail, but big on ideas. And we had done very little to fill in the detail when, a few months later, I put most of my belongings into storage and got into an old Toyota van that had previously housed a smelly, wind-swept hippie couple.

I ended the rental agreement with Amber. It all made perfect, beautiful sense to me at the time. Amber, like any good sister, remained mute. We wouldn't live together again. Not renewing the lease was a decision I later regretted.

The van cost about five grand, and we split it 50–50. At the time, two and a half thousand dollars was all of my savings. Dani was working as a waitress, and I had been doing some marking work at the uni for Donna and making no money on the independent theatre scene in Brisbane. The day we bought the van felt like we were putting a stake in the ground. We were serious. There was no turning back. It was a major investment, quite literally, in a shared future.

Dani christened the van 'The Gutless Wonder' or 'Gutsy' for short, not taking on Amber's suggested name 'Urine', after its uninspiring colour.

It was wild. There was endless possibility ahead of us.

'I just wanted to make sure you didn't want to take on another marking contract,' Donna emailed a few days before I left.

No need! I had the open road! People fruit pick, don't they? Don't know how that works, but that'll cover our fuel and food. No contract, thank you!

'I just want you to be sure you're not changing who you are to make someone else happy,' Amber said quietly before we departed.

No! This is exactly who I am. Don't you see? After all this time? I'm free now! I'm on the open road with the woman I love!

'Have you got insurance? Has a mechanic looked it over?' Mum asked me over the phone.

Ah, we can't afford that. But I'm sure it will be fine. I know how to fix a flat tyre! It's an adventure!

Convinced of success and with a thousand dollars

between us we set out, heading west.

Day one. We were to meet a friend in St George, about six hours out of Brisbane. A day's drive. An easy goal to reach on our first day.

∧∧∧

We're an hour from St George when we hear the noise. It's a loud 'pop'.

'Was that us?' Dani asks.

I do a thorough mechanical assessment of the situation by turning around in my seat and looking around the interior of the car, before briefly looking over the road in front of us.

'I think we're okay.'

Less than thirty seconds later, Dani is sounding quite alarmed: 'The temperature gauge is going up. I think the engine's overheating.'

She barely gets to the end of the sentence before smoke emerges from the front of the van, and we hear another loud pop from somewhere behind us.

I know enough about engines to understand that overheating is not a great thing. We pull over into the red dust at the side of the road.

I get out and lift up the passenger seat to find the curious mess of an engine that's as hot as sin.

'What do we do?' Dani asks.

I shrug.

'I guess we wait for it to cool down.'

It's the middle of the afternoon. We're an hour outside St George, which roughly translates as the middle of nowhere. A straight road leads into the distance ahead and behind us, and the quiet dry hum of empty bushland surrounds us.

I did my best to remember that we were having an adventure.

We wait for about an hour by the side of the road for the engine to cool. When we continue driving, we only go a couple of kilometres before the same thing happens. The engine is boiling. We pull over again, wait for a while, and then I carefully remove the radiator cap. We have a three-litre bottle of water in the back for just these sorts of occasions. (We were prepared, after all.) The van glugged down all three litres with furious thirst.

Right. That should solve the problem.

This time we made it another five kilometres before we had to pull over. We went through the same routine again, except this time we poured our bottles of drinking water into the radiator. The sun was now setting, and we'd given up all of our water.

After another couple of k's we pulled over again. It had been two hours since we'd first stopped and we'd only travelled about ten kilometres.

I tried to assess the situation. 'So we're out of phone reception.'

'Yep.'

'Out of water.'

'Yep.'

'The sun is setting.'

'Yep.'

'And we can only move a few k at a time.'

'Yep. Maybe. I don't know. Maybe it's too dangerous to drive at all.'

We looked at each other blankly, hoping the other would be able to provide some answer. But one never came.

We had no other choice: we had to abandon the van. I stood by the side of the highway and stuck out my thumb. Over a period of twenty minutes, I almost got run down by two huge trucks, but at last a ute pulled into the dirt behind us. A tall middle-aged man with greying hair got out and made a quick assessment.

Our radiator, he kindly informed us, was busted, and without a tow we'd have to stop to refill the radiator every ten k or so to get Gutsy to St George. She was in desperate need of a mechanic.

So we got to St George ten k at a time, with the kind man following us the whole way. He was a local, and he knew the creeks. He'd run off into the bush to fill his water up and then fill up our radiator fresh each time we stopped. What should've been a one-hour drive took about five. When we finally got to St George and pulled into our friend's place, the man waved goodbye and kept going.

I don't know his name, and I've never seen him since.

Gutsy was dead. And our dreams with it.

The call from the mechanic came twenty-four hours later.

'Are you sitting down?' he asked.

'I am now,' I said.

Across the room, Dani was looking at me, hopefully.

'It's dead mate. Radiator's gone and the entire engine needs to be refitted. You're looking at over five thousand to fix it, which is probably more than it's worth.'

'Yeah, okay.'

When I tell Dani the news, she cries. The mechanic tows Gutsy to our friend's backyard. We need to make a plan to dump it or fix it. Either way, we catch a lift back to Brisbane. We're homeless and poor.

We crashed at a friend's place and spent the summer in poverty and crippling heat. We reluctantly went back to work. Dani's crystalline dream was shattered, and our future was blank.

I struggled to keep up a sense of calm. I collapsed into anxiety. Dani nursed me through panic attacks as we couch-hopped from her sister's to various friend's. I had never been homeless before, and the lack of routine and stability left me out of my mind. It felt like we were drifting without an anchor. Similarly, Dani was staring down the barrel of several more months of hard hospitality work to restore her savings. I nursed her through tears and despair.

Meanwhile, Gutsy was still out at St George. But I had a mate. Or rather, a husband of a mate, who knew engines better than most, and he figured we could rebuild it. Ted was married to Donna, my lecturer at uni. I had remained in close contact with Donna and babysat for her regularly.

Ted accompanied me on what turned out to be an eighteen-hour-straight round trip to collect the van. We towed the sad thing right into Ted's driveway in Brisbane. And Ted and I spent the summer rebuilding the engine from the inside out.

When I asked Dani if she wanted to come and help, she said she felt awkward and didn't want to get in the way. I nodded that it was fine, but inside I was resentful. My desire to keep her happy won out, however, and I didn't express my annoyance. But we stopped talking in any meaningful way. I suddenly resented everything I had given up and how much I had changed, and I could see that Dani felt guilty. We both spiralled into negativity. But I was determined to keep the relationship alive. I couldn't afford to lose it. Not now, not after all this. Besides, I loved her. And, after all, wasn't that all we needed?

I learnt about oil, crankshafts and radiators from the type of man who I wanted to become: whip-smart, family-centred, a beautiful husband and father. He was the masculine ideal. And he was friendly and very kind to me. We shared a taste for pop culture and became friends. Within three months, and costing another hard-earned thousand dollars in parts and a lot of sweat, Gutsy was running again. The hard summer was nearly over, and a new year was underway.

We had spent the last nine months chasing Dani's dream, and with it now dashed, I stood up to take control as I thought a man should. I tried to design a life Dani could be happy with.

Dani, who had previously trained in teaching and dressmaking, would become an actress, and the two of us would return to our hometown to make a new start. I went back to the same university to teach. Donna, with her endless generosity, gave me work. And Dani enthusiastically studied acting.

We spent a lot of nights indoors, watching TV. Our conversations got smaller; our shadows grew larger. Our hearts that had once beat so quickly grew withered and slow.

When Dani said one day that she wanted to leave I begged her to stay. And she did, for another three months or so. But it was no good. It wasn't going to work.

We were unhappy for many months, and we stayed in that unhappiness because we were too scared to move. We didn't even talk about it.

I'm surprised we lasted as long as we did. We were two fundamentally different individuals. Dani is a gorgeous person; she taught me all kinds of things about myself that I didn't know. It was a real and significant relationship for both of us. But, without knowing it, I had fallen into the exact same trap that I had throughout my entire life. Not Crazy Drama Dave, not Gay Dave, but this time 'Dani's Boyfriend Dave'. It was a role I had taken on with so much seriousness, it doomed the relationship right from the start. Lovingly light and airy Dani was chained down by my neediness and fear.

We were standing in the kitchen over bowls of cereal. There was no sound but for the crunching of our breakfast.

'I think I don't want to be in this relationship anymore,' she said.

I nodded, slowly. I wasn't surprised.

'But I love you,' she said into the silence.

'I love you too,' I replied.

'We'll be friends.'

'We can keep trying,' I said, but even I was not convinced.

Dani shook her head. 'I don't think it's meant to be.'

I left the house and the van and I escaped to Brisbane. I was unsure if I was moving forward, or perpetually moving backward. I kept moving as quickly as possible, because I was too afraid to stop.

I was single again. I had lost Dani again. I was in this same mental place. Again.

I found a single bedroom on the ground floor of the lush apartment of a happy couple who lived upstairs. I sank into loneliness.

My memories of the break-up became warped. I was convinced that Dani had fallen out of love with me. But I was hanging onto her for dear life—how could you just fall out of love with someone? Perhaps we could try an open relationship? Or a six-month break?

I was in the void again, and the darkness enveloped me more than ever before. I ignored all my past knowledge of how to help myself. I was so tired. It seemed I would never escape the endless cycle I was trapped in.

Why bother going to a psychologist and getting up off the mat again? I'd had a good run, I reasoned. But I couldn't be bothered piecing back my identity and putting it into something that would no doubt give way once more. Every time I tried to rebuild myself I ended up in this awful place.

At the end of the year, I made a concrete plan to end my own life. And I set about putting it into action.

18

Too Far Gone

Killing yourself is not as easy as you might think. It takes commitment and a great deal of planning to do it 'right'.

For example, imagine for a moment you get it *wrong*, and you wake up in a hospital. Then you're that person. You're the guy who tried to kill himself. I didn't want to have to face up to my parents or friends and explain why. I didn't want everyone watching over me like a hawk for years afterwards. Any time I slipped into a bad mood I'd have to be placed on 'watch'.

Worse, what if I only cleared out my consciousness? I imagined my body, thin and pale, under the harsh fluorescence of hospital lights, the soft mechanical beep of a machine promising something that the rest of my body wasn't. 'Yes, I am still alive!' But only just. My mother giving the nod to pull the plug. How awful. I fail to kill myself and force my mother to become a murderer? There are few grander ways to fail as a human being than to put your loved ones in that position.

Similarly, I didn't particularly want friends, family or even acquaintances finding my body. This would be too much of a trauma to leave them with.

I thought a lot about everyone around me. I can't say it's the case for all suicidal people, but it was certainly true for me: I didn't doubt that people cared. I didn't wish to leave the planet because I wasn't loved enough. No amount of fierce loving would've made me any better.

It was me. I hated me. I hated the black and endless void inside of me. I was bound up in regret and anxiety and nothingness. I had placed my trust in structures that had slipped out of my hands with heartbreaking fluidity. High school. Sexuality. A girlfriend. All of these things were gone. It didn't occur to me once to place faith in myself, to figure out who I was—because I was no one. I had no identity. The only thing there was black emptiness.

And so I told myself I needed to die.

My mind became obsessed with death. Every ceiling beam became an opportunity to end it all. I saw my body hanging limp, swaying gently from a rope as my soul dissolved into thin air.

It wasn't necessarily the method that bothered me. Hanging seemed okay. Possible. A gun was the easiest and quickest. If I had been able to purchase a gun, I probably would have. Drowning was equally possible. A poet's death. But I was scared my body would betray me, that the end would come too slowly, that I would fight my way to the surface at the last minute, hating myself all the more.

Still, it was a possibility. The method wasn't difficult, it was finding a space that was private enough to carry it out.

I thought of pills, tiny bottles of poison, neat in their finality. But the execution of a drug overdose again may have ended up with my body fighting back. My weak stomach would likely vomit the whole lot up, and what if I only ended up brain dead?

The thoughts circulated and became coldly precise and deliberate. Planning, figuring it out, looking at how. It seemed only a matter of time. Occasionally, I would have a moment of lucidity, like waking from some terrible nightmare, and then I'd realise that something was terribly wrong. I shouldn't be thinking this. I needed to do something.

Talking to Gary seemed too painful. What was the point? I would only end up here in the same void again.

There was one option that I'd never tried before. And I figured there was nothing to lose.

In the middle of our suburb was a run-down, over-worked medical centre. I had never been in before, but I called and made an appointment to see a GP.

I read a worn copy of *Woman's Day* in the waiting room, surrounded by coughing children and sleepy-eyed parents. In the corner was a Christmas tree. The tinny sound of popular carols leaked through the stereo system. It was December 22nd.

The young male doctor who called me into his office gave me a benign smile as I sat down.

'What can we do for you?'

I coughed, embarrassed. If I was going to say it I needed to say it. Just get this done.

'I, uh, I have a history of depression and I'm in the middle of a pretty intense, um...I don't know...'

The doctor nodded slowly.

'Are you thinking of hurting yourself?' he asked, neutrally.

I looked down. 'Um, yeah.'

'Have you done anything to hurt yourself?'

'Not yet.'

'Are you alone?'

I was puzzled at that question. What did he mean? Living alone? No friends? I didn't understand.

Yes I'm alone! I wanted to scream at him. I'm fucking terrifyingly pants-shittingly alone!!

'Um, I've got, um, friends and that.' (Of course, Amber, Ravi and Donna had no idea about what was going on.)

'Okay,' the doctor nodded. He scribbled a note quickly on a prescription pad, tore it and handed it to me.

'Have you been on antidepressants before?' he asked.

'No.'

'Take one of these a day, just before bed. They'll make you drowsy.'

That was the entire interaction. I was out of the office within four minutes.

Puzzled, I called Gary. I wanted to know what the pill was, how it was going to affect me, and if it was addictive. He did some quick research and called me back.

'If you feel like you need it, take it,' he said. 'But you should know that there have been some reported cases of it increasing suicidal thoughts, particularly in young men. If you feel like you need it to get you through Christmas, take it. But watch yourself, and you should book an appointment with me.'

We said goodbye and I hung up, more confused. Did I need it? What if it made things worse? Was it possible to overdose on these things and finish myself off?

Without thinking, I rang Mum and Dad. After small talk, I explained I had been to a GP.

'Just to help me out. You know. The break-up. I've got some pills here.'

'Oh, Dave,' said Dad, 'I think that's the right decision, mate. You need to look after yourself.'

'Come home,' said Mum. 'Come home and take the pills and get better.'

I shrugged it off. 'It's no big deal,' I said.

We said our goodbyes.

That night, alone in my bedroom, I swallowed a single pill with water. It was 7pm. Half an hour later, I was soundly asleep. I disappeared inside a forgiving blackness.

A vibration at my hip stirred me. I felt as though I had gained a hundred kilos. My entire body was heavy, every muscle was lead. I breathed deep, and strained to open my eyes. The light seemed to burn me. I reached for my phone.

It was Dani. Dani was calling me.

'Hello?' I said. My voice was dry and crackly.

'Hey,' she said.

Silence.

My brain was moving too slowly to speak. I didn't know what to say. It was daylight. What time was it?

'Are you okay?' A voice came from the other end of the line. Dani was on the phone. Dani was calling me, I'd forgotten...

'I'm, uh...' my voice trailed off.

'Dave?'

'I've taken this pill, this antidepressant thing, um.' What time was it?

'Oh.' Her voice was heavy with recognition.

I was still in my clothes from the day before.

'I'll speak to you later,' I said. I hung up the phone and checked the time. It was 11.30am.

As I slumped my way to the shower, the world around me seemed to shift and change. I felt as though my soul had left my body. Every movement took a strength and an energy that I didn't possess.

I stood in the shower and let the hot water course over my body, all the time praying. Please God, please, if you have any kindness, just kill me. Just leave me alone. Please, please, please, let me die.

I went back to bed. It was the only thing I had any energy to do. If there had been a gun, or even a knife within reaching distance, I would've used it.

But there wasn't, so I slept for the afternoon.

When I woke up, slowly coming out of the drug,

I knew I wouldn't be taking it again. There would be no need. I would only live for a few more days.

∿∿∿

After much thought, I arrived at a firm conclusion. A car. It made sense. I was too much of a coward to stab myself, and I knew that drowning would result in me swimming to the shore and vomiting up sea water. My cowardice became another reason for my self-hatred. But gassing myself in my hatchback seemed to be an appropriate end.

I had been considering it for some time. On a final trip to reclaim my things from the house I shared with Dani, I had stolen a garden hose and hidden it in the back of my car. It had been there for weeks, waiting for me to make the final act.

I put a pile of old towels on the back seat. These would help with the circulation of the fumes. I had seen on television that you were supposed to line the windows and doors with towels, to make sure none of the poisonous gas escaped or became diluted.

Not wanting to ruin Christmas forever for those I was leaving behind, I vowed to hold on for another week. I spent it with my extended family, and then I had a couple of days with Mum and Dad.

The time with them made me feel some guilt. I

needed to make sure I had done everything I could to find happiness again.

I went to see Dani one more time to plead my case.

We met at a coffee shop. I was taken aback by what I found. Dani was joyous, relaxed and free. She was a different woman from the one I had come to know in the last six months of our relationship. She was happy.

'I'd forgotten how much I *loved* men!' she squealed, laughing, telling me of the pleasure she was finding in being able to flirt again.

Even in my sadness, I realised that this was the way it had to be. Dani was just being Dani, and I couldn't ask her to be anything other than who she was. I had to let her go. She was already gone. There was no going back.

I had seen my friends that day also. We had played boardgames at Ted's house. I had the opportunity to speak to Amber. I had a brother and sister there, with ears to listen. It didn't matter. I was too far gone.

My car was ready.

I was ready.

This was it.

Outside my Brisbane home, I sat in the front seat of my car and tried to think of where I could go to park the car and be alone. Outside, the rain was pouring down, and I wondered how this would affect the fumes. It was late afternoon. I would find a spot, perhaps my beloved wheatfield that I had dreamed of all those years ago, and drift off into the sunset.

I googled my method on my phone. I wanted to make sure I was doing it right. As the sun set, the rain got heavier, and the sky turned dark grey. The bright screen blinked back at me and I saw my plan for suicide slowly melt away in the rain. My romantic vision of a field disappeared. I'd need an enclosed space for the fumes to work. I would have to make peace with the thought of the kind couple who lived upstairs finding me in their garage.

That made matters more difficult.

A quick scan of Wikipedia brought up other problems. Cars made after the 1970s have a catalytic converter installed in them, which drastically reduces the toxicity of their fumes. My car was made in 2000. Unleaded and ethanol fuels were dramatically ineffective. I had, of course, filled my car with ethanol fuel.

Dammit.

I started the car and drove. I drove for two hours. The road was slick with wet, and I contemplated the vision of my crumpled car careering off the highway. But unless I put myself into the path of another vehicle, I couldn't guarantee my own demise. And I didn't want to traumatise some innocent truck driver. I was trying desperately to think of a nice and generous way to kill myself.

No such thing exists. You cannot erase the marks you leave behind.

I found myself, almost without thinking, at my parents' doorstep.

It was midnight by the time I pulled in. Uncharacteristically, my father was still up. I didn't realise it, but I was crying. I had been crying for hours.

'I'm fine,' I insisted as I sobbed.

Dad nodded. I hadn't cried in front of him for years. The rest of the house was still and quiet.

'Dave,' he said, 'What's up?'

In the close darkness of the lounge room, with a Bond film on mute, I whispered my pain through tears.

'I don't understand,' I kept saying. 'I just want her.'

Dad nodded. He'd had a girlfriend before Mum. He had felt the same way about her. I never even knew that.

'I know this is awful,' he said, 'and there's nothing that I can say to make it go away. I can only tell you that it gets better with time. If you get through this, if you overcome this, you'll never look back. This'll be the making of you.'

I went to bed in the wee small hours.

I had survived the day.

19

How to Be Unhappy

'The first thing you need to do is realise how serious this is.' Gary's face was stern. 'You're in the middle of a severe depressive episode. If you don't take meaningful steps to help your recovery, then we really need to make decisions. You may need to be hospitalised.'

Right. Wow. Okay.

Hospitalised?

I imagined myself in a white room, in a white bed, with white furniture. It would feel nice to not have control over my own life anymore, to give up any sense of responsibility. But the embarrassment would be too painful to bear.

'I just feel so alone,' I found myself saying.

'Do you have friends to talk to?' he asked.

I started to list off my mates.

Amber.

Ravi.

Nina.

Donna and Ted.

I was going to continue, but Gary's relieved laughter interrupted the list.

'You need to talk to these people,' he said. 'Most people in your position are very much alone. They have difficulty building long-lasting or meaningful relationships. You need to use the support you've been given. That's your homework for this week.'

When I walked out of the Gary's office that night, Ravi and Nina were waiting for me on the kerb. Nina was clutching a hot water bottle and complaining of period pain. Ravi was smoking a cigarette. He gave me a hug. We went to a park, got lost in the dark, and played on the play equipment like we were children again. It had been raining all day, but it had cleared as the moon rose. I raced to the top of a slide, encouraged by Ravi.

'Wait,' I yelled out once I was at the top. 'Is it wet down the bottom?'

There was a brief pause.

'No,' came the reply from them both.

I went for it and landed with a large splash at the bottom.

My pants were soaked. I looked like I had shat myself. We laughed a lot.

On our way back, the three of us traipsed into a service station. Ravi's car was precariously low on fuel and Ravi was low on funds. He was wearing sunglasses, despite the fact that it was pitch-black night. Nina was clutching her hot water bottle and nursing her head. I was thin, gaunt, and looked like I'd had a burst of diarrhoea down the back of my pants.

The gormless young man at the counter didn't know what to make of us as we fought over which ice-cream we would buy with our small handful of change. We lined up at the counter, and Ravi inserted his card into the machine.

He turned to me, and muttered out of the corner of his mouth, 'Fingers crossed everybody.'

I burst into giggles. This was the funniest thing I had ever heard. Seconds later, Ravi and Nina were giggling too. The look of concern on the man's face only made it worse, and we sputtered out of the place.

I laughed for a very long time. I hadn't laughed properly in months.

We found ourselves on top of the water tower, a place we had visited regularly back in uni days, bringing fish and chips or some other greasy dinner. The city was quiet below us. Somewhere out there, I thought, are people just like me. People who are ending their own lives. Or people who feel the pressure slowly mounting, pushing them towards breaking point. Those people are not on top of a water tower with two friends beside them.

So I breathed deep and I told Nina and Ravi everything.

Ravi said nothing. He just hugged me. It was a very long, very strong hug.

Nina took a moment. And then she looked me in the eye. 'If you had done that,' she began, 'I wouldn't have been able to forgive you. I don't think I would've been able to go to your funeral. That's a cowardly thing to do David, and you're not a coward. You're better than that. Don't do that kind of bullshit.'

I nodded. Her reaction surprised me and shook me. I've thought of her words often in the time since.

For the umpteenth time in my life, I told my friends and family that I hadn't been entirely honest with them. But this confession was far more awful than an admission of sexuality. I didn't feel anxiety this time. I felt shame. Nina's response, and Gary's laughter, made me realise just how closed off I had been.

Donna and I went out to dinner. I didn't know how to tell her, I proposed the whole thing like an absurdist joke. 'And *then* I realised that I couldn't GAS myself! Typical!'

Donna's eyes became hollow and sad. She said, very quietly, 'You know Dave, if you ever did that, I'd have to tell my sons what had happened to you. They love you a lot, Dave. Please don't make me do that.'

Yes. Fair enough.

I couldn't bring myself to tell Amber. I was deeply ashamed that I hadn't talked to her properly. But like all good sisters, she understood, and she began a fierce campaign to provide support for me.

It was the small things, in that time, that helped. Like midnight visits to a playground, or a trip to the movies, or a phone call to talk about bullshit. I didn't really want to talk about what was happening with me. I didn't want anyone to look at me with pity and say, 'So, how *are* you?' That was the quickest way to get me to retreat. It was just about my mates being my mates, and just being around. That helped. That saved my life.

〰〰

I moved back home with Mum and Dad and the twins. Not having to worry about rent or food released enough pressure in my head for me to start thinking about how I might avoid ending up in a dark place again.

For the first time since I was thirteen, I wasn't consumed with concern about making sure I was liked and popular. I wasn't worried about finding a new personality. I knew I wouldn't lose Ravi, Amber and Nina. They were good friends who had my back. I didn't have to worry about pleasing them. My parents graciously accepted me back into the house. I had support.

But I had been on the other side of this relationship a few times before. I had tried furiously to fix Mary, and had only run myself into the ground in the process. I knew the ultimate responsibility for my wellbeing lay with me. I needed to get myself better.

I picked up a new teaching contract and a couple of paying theatre projects.

I wandered through daily life in a quiet daze, not quite sure how I had ended up back in a house with my family.

I usually woke up earlier than anyone else in the house, just as the sun was rising. I would drag myself to the kitchen and flick the kettle on. A cup of tea later, I would sit down to emails and daily business. I may have had some meetings later in the day, but I was usually done with the majority of my work by ten in the morning. I would prepare another cup of tea, turn on the radio, and listen to the ABC while I completed three or four sudoku puzzles. There was something about this little morning routine that kept me calm. I felt my brain slow down into a natural hushed rhythm.

By early afternoon, I would become slightly restless. I needed to put my energy into something. I went in search of a complicated recipe. Layered chocolate cakes. Gnocchi in a special sauce. Golden-syrup dumplings. I put the audiobook of *Eat Pray Love* on my iPod and made an utter mess of the kitchen. By the end of the afternoon I had built a bizarre menu. Some dishes were fantastic successes, others were dismal failures. The end result didn't bother me that much. I was grateful that my hands and mind had been kept busy.

In the evening I'd have a glass of wine with dinner, but this was my only consumption of alcohol. By virtue of the fact that I was living with my family, I'd also abandoned my occasional pot use.

Overall, life felt simple and calm. I felt alone—but it wasn't scary.

Actually, it was kind of nice.

Happiness was a concept that still confused me, but I certainly felt peaceful. Anxiety dripped away while I built this little routine for myself. It took a lot of time.

Many days were boring. There were shit days too.

One evening, when the rest of the house had gone to bed, I was mindlessly flicking through Facebook. Dani had been tagged in a video. The play button stared back at me, waiting to be pressed. I could see from the blurry still image that I was unlikely to enjoy what I saw. It was Dani on a dark dance floor, with a man nearby.

I should turn off my computer and go to bed, I thought.

I hit play.

Dani danced, slow and flirtatious, with a man I didn't recognise. Music thumped in the background. Whoever had the camera was laughing. It was thirty seconds long.

My breath shortened. I felt like throwing up. My skin pricked alive. I wanted to rip it off. I needed to punch something. Or myself. Or that guy in the video. I wanted to scream, but I couldn't wake the house. I wasn't even thinking about the video now. I just felt pain. Hot, red pain through my entire body.

I lay on the floor, curled into a ball, and sobbed.

∿∿∿

'Okay, and what happened next?'

Gary sat across from me, legs crossed. I shifted in my seat as I thought back.

'I stayed there for a while, and then I went to bed.'

'How did you feel afterwards?'

'Empty. Exhausted.'

Gary nods. 'Sounds like you had a panic attack.'

'Just from seeing a video?' I asked, disappointed.

'That's so pathetic.'

'Is that something you tell yourself often?'

'What?'

'That you're pathetic?'

I pause for a moment. 'Yes,' I said.

'What else do you tell yourself?'

'Um...' I close my eyes. The question makes me uncomfortable. Maybe if I'm quiet for long enough he'll ask something else. But there's nothing. That plan never works. Gary has patience plus. I sigh and attempt to answer. 'I think I'm weak...I don't know...um...pathetic's a pretty big one.'

Gary nods for a moment before speaking. 'I think it's important for you to start recognising what you've been through. You don't strike me as a weak person. You strike me as someone who spends a lot of time beating himself up. Would you agree?'

I'm not sure where this is going. 'I...yeah...I don't know.'

'You spend a lot of time thinking about things you *should* be doing, or punishing yourself for not living up to some expectation.'

'But it's pretty pathetic, isn't it? One video and I have a panic attack? It's been three months. I should be over her by now.'

'Says who?'

I shrug. 'I don't know. Me.'

Gary smiles. 'Let me put it to you this way. If you had Amber or Ravi come up to you and say they'd been through all of this—that they'd been through a break-up, that they'd been diagnosed with depression and anxiety, felt sad enough to want to kill themselves and then they'd had a panic attack from watching a video of their ex—what would you say to them? Would you say they were pathetic?'

Godammit. He had a point.

'No,' I relented.

'So why are you holding yourself to that standard?'

Silence. I didn't have an answer for him.

'David, you need to give yourself permission to feel certain things. You've been running away from your feelings for a long time. A very long time. You're in a safe place where you're allowed to actually process some of those emotions. However that happens is okay. You've got to let it come out. Otherwise you won't ever get through to the other side.'

I ran a hand through my hair. I was frustrated. He made it sound so easy.

'It's hard.'

Gary nodded. 'Yeah, it really is. But you're capable of it. You're not weak.'

'I feel weak.'

'You can't fight this kind of thing. Wouldn't you agree?'

'What do you mean?'

'You've spent a lot of time fighting how you feel. How has that fight gone so far?'

'Not great.'

'The fight is exhausting. In order to get through this kind of thing you have to give yourself permission to feel it.'

He had uncrossed his legs and was leaning forward. He was really trying to make this clear to me. It kind of made sense. Was that really all there was to it? I just had to surrender to all the feelings inside me?

'How do I actually do that? And isn't it dangerous?' I asked.

'Well, do you want to kill yourself anymore?'

I thought for a moment. The dark thoughts hadn't had a violent intensity ever since I had shared them with Donna, Ravi and Nina. 'No,' I replied.

'Well then,' he said. 'What are you going to do next?'

〰〰

It's six months later, and Nina and I are driving to go get some lunch.

'When are you going to move out of your parents' place?' she asked.

I hadn't thought about it. The free rent made life easy. But in the last few weeks I had found the lack of privacy more and more irritating. Maybe I was ready to move out again.

'I could move out!' I said aloud, thinking about it properly for the first time.

'Yeah,' Nina laughed. 'You could.'

Later, Amber and Ravi applauded the idea. But all of my friends were tied up in lease agreements. I would have to live by myself.

The idea was instantly alluring. A whole place to myself. Independent. Not defined by anybody. Mine.

I found a flat that I loved on the other side of town, packed up and moved. On my first night there, Ravi, Amber and Nina came around. We watched reality television and ate roast chicken that I made in my very own oven. Then they went home. And I washed up and went to bed.

I wish I could tell you it was more dramatic than that. But I was done with drama. A peaceful and normal evening with friends and without anxiety was something I thought I could never reach. Now I had found it, I never wanted to go back.

∿∿∿

My biggest achievement during that time was learning how to be unhappy. You would think I had become an expert at this, but in fact I'd been doing it all wrong.

Sometimes, unhappiness is near impossible to avoid. Bad things happen. And it's important to be sad. It doesn't make you weak.

Of course it wasn't as simple as my psychologist snapping his fingers and giving me permission to feel emotions. We spent a lot of time talking about mindfulness, a practice where you train your brain to sit in stillness. I studied meditation. I tried to develop a habit of exercise. I constantly pushed myself to be more honest about what I was feeling with myself and my friends.

Important questions still remained.

Without high school, without uni, without a relationship—who was I? Who was I when nobody was watching?

Gradually, the thought of myself alone in the void didn't scare me anymore. It didn't send me running for a new relationship, label or career. I was able to find peace within it. I came to terms with my unhappiness. It didn't have such a dangerous grip on me anymore. It took a whole lot of time and a whole bunch of work. But I was up for it. I wanted to be happy. I was sick of feeling awful. I chose to do what I could to find happiness.

∿∿∿

I'm twenty-two. I sit alone in my unit. I've just showered. I have cookbooks open around me. I'm deciding what I'll make today. I have a deadline for a script that I'll dash off soon, before running over to the theatre and taking a youth drama class. It's Amber's birthday in a week, and I need to answer the Facebook stream and make a final decision for a celebratory venue.

Beside me, my phone rings.

I briefly think about not picking it up. For a moment, the day seems a bit too much. There's a lot to do. I could crawl into bed and hide for the day, put off my work until tomorrow.

The phone could be someone I'm working for. It could be a parent wanting to know about this afternoon's class. Or the theatre producer giving me new notes on the script. The thought sends a shiver of anxiety through me. Will today be the day people start realising I'm not good enough?

It could be Ravi. Or Amber.

Do I really want to participate in the world today?

Am I strong enough to be a functional human being? To participate? To exist?

I think for a moment.

Tomorrow I might need to retreat. And that'll be okay.

But today, I'm making the choice to show up. I know I have that strength today.

I pick up the phone.

Now

At time of writing, it's been fifteen years since Cameron pushed me over that visual arts table. It's been five years since I moved out of home for the second time. Life has carried on.

Dani completed her acting degree, and is in the middle of building an amazing career as one of the most interesting theatre artists in the country. We don't talk much, but we see each other now and then.

I'm still very close with Ted and Donna. Donna's role at the university developed to a leadership position. I cannot tell you the number of people I've met in the arts and education sectors who tell me, unprompted, that Donna changed their lives at university. Donna has only the vaguest idea of how she affects her students. Ted continues to be an outstanding father, husband and friend. I still occasionally babysit their two boys.

Amber is having an amazing career as one of the most influential arts producers in Queensland. We are still best friends.

James had a long-term boyfriend for many years, and is in the middle of an exploding career. He lives with Amber, and we talk and work together regularly.

Ravi splits his time between Australia and Korea, where he teaches and does amazing work with disenfranchised youth. He remains one of the most remarkable human beings I've ever met. We're still best friends.

Nina became a high-school teacher. She remains one of the smartest people I know, and one of the greatest teachers I've ever seen in a classroom. We're not as close as we used to be, but we still talk from time to time.

Immediately after our time together, Rachel had several

serious relationships with women. We've fallen out of contact.

Tiff and I managed to reconnect a few years back when our professional lives intersected. She's the proud mother of a new baby, and is happily married.

After a decade of having never said goodbye, an intensive Facebook search finally uncovered Mary. She lives far away. I messaged her and we had a brief conversation, both expressing our happiness at the other's adult life. Mary is well, and she is a mother. We haven't talked since.

A quick Facebook search reveals Cameron to be a concrete labourer, and happily in love.

I don't know where Ray is.

I don't know where Simon is.

Mum and Dad have both retired. They have health issues, both mental and physical, but are happy most of the time. After a few years of unsettled communication, we finally got around to figuring out how to have a grown child–older parent relationship. I talk to them regularly.

Andy and Chrissy still live with Mum and Dad. I don't talk to them often, but we have a happy relationship.

After a few months of living by myself, I asked a very lovely woman named Emily out on a date. We had worked together on a play.

When I texted her asking for a coffee, she said yes. The coffee became lunch, and we ended up talking for five hours. It was the easiest conversation I had ever had.

Emily's the best thing that ever happened to me. She's one of the greatest humans I've ever met. I'm grateful for her every day.

After being together for a couple of years, we got married. Amber was best man. Ravi was a grooms-man. My brothers made a speech that made everyone cry, even though it was entirely harvested from popular culture. It was one of the best days of my life. Our families came together and danced and laughed.

Quite unexpectedly, I find myself with a life that I never thought I deserved.

∿∿∿

I can't tell you how to be happy.

Sometimes, I still struggle. I still have periods where I suffer from anxiety and depression.

But I'm also happy a lot of the time.

It happens without warning.

I'm baking a cake and listening to an audiobook. I'm solving a sudoku puzzle. I'm laughing with my friends over a boardgame. I'm sitting with Emily and talking about our plans for the day.

And then, quietly, and with the most delicious lightness, a feeling gently taps me on the shoulder.

It's something deep and familiar. It's something of air. A fragile energy.

It's happiness. Staring back at me, and smiling. It's a version of myself that I never thought I'd find.

I'm not always great at this, but I try to take a moment and breathe. To smile at it. Nod hello.

Yes, I am happy.

Yes, this is good.

Yes, life is okay.

Then I go about my day.

I carry on living.

Acknowledgments

A debut work isn't born in a vacuum, and this little baby has had a whole lot help from some very smart, very gracious people.

Firstly, a very important thanks to Dan McMahon. Dan, when you asked me to come and talk to your year-twelve students about growing up I was sceptical that I had a story worth sharing. Your belief in my voice is the fundamental reason this book exists. Thank you for your confidence.

There are many people who read the book at various stages and gave me critical opinions at critical times. Huge thanks to Neridah Waters, Liesel Zink, Travis

Dowling, Margi Brown-Ash, Susan Mackenzie and Jason Klarwein. Your encouragement was invaluable.

Thank you also to the handful of people who are *in* this book, who read it and gave me their gracious blessing. I am very grateful.

How on earth do I even begin to thank Text Publishing for their belief and support? I'm honoured to be a Text author. Special thanks to my editor, Jane Pearson, for being downright amazing.

To my friends—most of you read the book at different times or lived the experience with me. To Claire, Ari, Steve, Carley, Janet, Richard, I am nowhere without you.

Thank you to Mum, Dad, Andy and Chrissy. Thanks for trusting me with a small piece of our story, and thank you for raising a neurotic young man so gracefully.

Finally, thanks for being an amazing wife, Em, and for believing in me and the book. I love you.

IF YOU NEED HELP

∿∿

Lifeline 13 11 14

Kids Helpline 1800 55 1800

∿∿

On the day that I cried for three hours while washing up the dishes, I called a crisis support line. They really helped get me through another day. If you're feeling like you've got nowhere else to turn, give them a ring. You've got nothing to lose by doing it.

CPSIA information can be obtained
at www.ICGtesting.com
Printed in the USA
LVOW03s0903211117
557073LV00006B/13/P